REMEMBER
WORDSWORTH

Essays and Extracts
on the
Life and Work
of the Great Poet

By

VARIOUS

Copyright © 2020 Ragged Hand

This edition is published by Ragged Hand,
an imprint of Read & Co.

This book is copyright and may not be reproduced or copied in any
way without the express permission of the publisher in writing.

British Library Cataloguing-in-Publication Data
A catalogue record for this book is available
from the British Library.

Read & Co. is part of Read Books Ltd.
For more information visit
www.readandcobooks.co.uk

"The best portion of a good man's life is his little, nameless, unremembered acts of kindness and of love."

—William Wordsworth

CONTENTS

"Fill your paper with the breathings of your heart."

—WILLIAM WORDSWORTH

WILLIAM WORDSWORTH.

By Hattie Tyng Griswold

Mr. Swinburne quotes the following passage from a description given by one of the daily papers of a certain murderer who at the time was attracting great attention in London:—

> "He has great taste for poetry, can recite long passages from popular poets,—Byron's denunciations of the pleasures of the world having for him great attraction as a description of his own experiences. Wordsworth is his favorite poet. He confesses himself a villain."

At this day the two latter facts will not necessarily be supposed to have any logical connection; but there was a time when the violence of the opponents of Wordsworth's claim to be a poet might have suggested the most intimate relation between these two statements. For many years he was looked upon as an "inspired idiot" by a large part of the reading world; and his place in literature has not been definitely settled to this day. Such extravagant claims have always been made for him by his friends that they have called forth just as extravagant denunciations from those who do not admire his works; and violent controversies arise concerning his merits among first-class scholars and critics. It is always noticeable, however, in these discussions that his panegyrists always quote his best efforts, those sublime passages to which no one denies transcendent merit, and that his opponents never get much beyond "Peter Bell," and other trivialities and absurdities, which his best friends must admit that he wrote in great numbers. That his best work ranks next to Shakespeare, Milton, and Shelley, can scarcely be doubted by any true lover of poetry; and he certainly has the right to be judged by his best, rather than by his inferior work.

Wordsworth was born in 1770, in Cumberland, and received his early education there, being noted for his excellence in classical studies and for his thoughtful disposition. He graduated from St. John's College, Cambridge, and immediately after began his literary labors, which were continued through a long and most industrious life.

In 1803 he married Miss Mary Hutchinson of Penrith, and settled at Grasmere, in Westmoreland, where he passed the remainder of his life, and where he lies buried in the little churchyard where so many of his family had preceded him. He helped to make the Lake district famous the world over, and himself never wearied of its charms. He was pre-eminently the poet of Nature, and it was from the unrivalled scenery of this part of England that he caught much of his inspiration. Mrs. Wordsworth, who was as fond of it as her husband, used to say in extreme old age, that the worst of living in the Lake region was that it made one unwilling to die when the time came. The poet's marriage was an eminently happy one, although Miss Martineau hints that it was not first love on his part, but that the lines, "She was a phantom of delight," so often quoted as relating to Mrs. Wordsworth, were really meant to indicate another person who had occupied his thoughts at an early day. At any rate, he did address the following lines to his wife after thirty-six years of married life, which is certainly a far higher compliment to her:—

"Morn into noon did pass, noon into eve,
And the old day was welcome as the young,
As welcome, and as beautiful,—in sooth, more beautiful,
As being a thing more holy."

The other poems, "Let other bards of angels sing," and "Oh,

dearer far than life and light are dear," were also addressed to her.

It was through her early friendship for Wordsworth's sister that she first came to know the poet, and she was not at that time a person whom a poet would be supposed to fancy. She was the incarnation of good-sense as applied to the concerns of the every-day world, and in no sense a dreamer, or a seeker after the ideal. Her intellect, however, developed by contact with higher minds, and her tastes after a time became more in accordance with those of her husband. She learned to passionately admire the outward world, in which he took such great delight, and to admire his poetry and that of his friends. She was of a kindly, cheery, generous nature, very unselfish in her dealings with her family, and highly beloved by her friends. She was the finest example of thrift and frugality to be found in her neighborhood, and is said to have exerted a decidedly beneficial influence upon all her poorer neighbors. She did not give them as much in charity as many others did, but she taught them how to take care of what they had, and to save something for their days of need. Miss Martineau, who was a neighbor, says: "The oldest residents have long borne witness that the homes of the neighbors have assumed a new character of order and comfort and wholesome economy, since the poet's family lived at Rydal Mount." She took the kindest and tenderest care of Wordsworth's sister Dorothy, who was for many years a helpless charge upon her hands. This sister had ruined her health, and finally dethroned her reason, by trying to accompany her brother on his long and tiresome rambles among the lakes and up the mountains. She has been known to walk with him forty miles in a single day. Many English women are famous walkers, but her record is beyond them all. Such excessive exercise is bad for a man, as was proved in the case of Dickens, who doubtless injured himself much by such long pedestrian trips after brain labor; but no woman can endure such a strain as this, and the adoring sister not only failed to be a companion to her idolized brother, but became a care and burden for many years. She lies now by her brother's side in the crowded little churchyard, and doubtless the "sweet bells jangled" are in tune again. A lovely group of children filled the Wordsworth home, some of whom died in childhood; but one daughter and two sons lived, as loving companions for their parents, until near the end of the poet's life, when the daughter Dora preceded him a little into the silent land. Wordsworth was utterly inconsolable for her loss; and used to spend the long winter evenings in tears, week after week, and month after month. Mrs. Wordsworth was much braver than he, and bore her own burdens calmly, while trying to cheer his exaggerated gloom. He was old and broken at this time, and never recovered from the shock of his daughter's death. Mrs. Wordsworth survived him for several years, being over ninety at the time of her death, and having long been deaf and blind. But she was very cheerful and active to the last, and not unwilling to live on, even with her darkened vision. The devotion of the old poet to his wife was very touching, and she who had idolized him in life was never weary of recounting his virtues when he was gone. The character of Wordsworth is getting to be understood as we recede from the prejudices of the time in which he lived, and begins to assume something like a consistent whole, compared to the contradictions which at one time seemed to be inherent in it. He says of his own childhood:—

> "I was of a stiff, moody, and violent temper; so much
> so that I remember going once into the attic of my
> grandfather's house at Penrith, upon some indignity
> having been put upon me, with an intention of destroying
> myself with one of the foils which I knew were kept
> there. I took the foil in my hand, but my heart failed."

De Quincey says of his boyhood:—

> "I do not conceive that Wordsworth could have been
> an amiable boy; he was austere and unsocial, I have
> reason to think, in his habits; not generous; and above

all, not self-denying. Throughout his later life, with all the benefits of a French discipline, in the lesser charities of social intercourse he has always exhibited a marked impatience of those particular courtesies of life. . . . Freedom,—unlimited, careless, insolent freedom,— unoccupied possession of his own arms,—absolute control over his own legs and motions,—these have always been so essential to his comfort that in any case where they were likely to become questionable, he would have declined to make one of the party."

Wordsworth has been accused of excessive penuriousness, of overwhelming conceit, and of being slovenly and regardless of dress. For the first accusation there seems little warrant, other than that he was prudent and thrifty, and knew the value of money. His most intimate friends exonerate him from meanness of any sort, and often praise his kindness to the poor and dependent. As regards conceit there can probably be no denial, though doubtless the stories told of it are much exaggerated. He is said never to have read any poetry but his own, and to have been exceedingly ill-natured and contemptuous in his estimate of his contemporaries. His estimate of Dickens is well known:—

"I will candidly avow that I thought him a very talkative, vulgar young person,—but I dare say he may be very clever. Mind, I don't want to say a word against him, for I have never read a word he has written."

He greeted Charles Mackay thus, when the latter called upon him:—

"I am told you write poetry. I never read a line of your poems and don't intend to. You must not be offended with me; the truth is, I never read anybody's poetry but my own."

Even James T. Fields, whose opinion of the poet was high, remarks:—

> "I thought he did not praise easily those whose names are indissolubly connected with his own in the history of literature. It was languid praise, at least; and I observed that he hesitated for mild terms which he could apply to names almost as great as his own."

Carlyle testifies on the same point:—

> "One evening, probably about this time, I got him upon the subject of great poets, who I thought might be admirable equally to us both; but was rather mistaken, as I gradually found. Pope's partial failure I was prepared for; less for the narrowish limits visible in Milton and others. I tried him with Burns, of whom he had sung tender recognition; but Burns also turned out to be a limited, inferior creature, any genius he had a theme for one's pathos rather; even Shakespeare himself had his blind sides, his limitations. Gradually it became apparent to me that of transcendent unlimited, there was to this critic probably but one specimen known,—Wordsworth."

As regards eccentricities of dress, we will give but a single testimony. William Jordan says:—

> "On his visits to town the recluse of Rydal Mount was quite a different creature. To me it was demonstrated, by his conduct under every circumstance, that De Quincey had done him gross injustice in the character he loosely threw upon him in public, namely, 'that he was not generous or self-denying, . . . and that he was slovenly and regardless in dress.' I must protest that there was no warrant for this caricature; but on the contrary, that

it bore no feature of resemblance to the slight degree of eccentricity discoverable in Cumberland, and was utterly contradicted by the life in London. In the mixed society of the great Babylon, Mr. Wordsworth was facile and courteous; dressed like a gentleman, and with his tall commanding figure no mean type of the superior order, well-trained by education, and accustomed to good manners. Shall I reveal that he was often sportive, and could even go the length of strong expressions, in the off-hand mirth of his observations and criticisms?"

Wordsworth had the fondness of many poets for reading his poetry to his friends, and even of reciting it like a schoolboy. When Emerson visited him he was already an old man, and it struck the philosopher so oddly, as he tells us in his "English Traits," to see "the old Wordsworth, standing apart, and reciting to me in a garden walk, like a schoolboy declaiming, that I at first was near to laugh; but recollecting myself, that I had come thus far to see a poet, and he was chanting poems to me, I saw that he was right and I was wrong, and gladly gave myself up to hear."

Another story is told of his being in a large company, and seeing for the first time a new novel by Scott, with a motto taken from his poems; and of his going immediately and getting the poem, and reading it entire to the assembled company, who were waiting for the reading of the new novel.

Literary biography is full of such anecdotes as these, going to show his absorption in himself, and his comparative indifference to the works of others; but they prove at most only a trifling weakness in a great man's character; such weaknesses being so common as to cause no surprise to those familiar with the lives of men of genius. He was a strong man, massive in his individuality, full of profound feeling and deep spirituality, and dominated by a powerful will. He was no mere sentimentalist and versifier, but a student at first hand of Nature and all her mysteries,—a man whose profound meditations had pierced to the centre of

15

things, and who held great thoughts in keeping for a waiting and expectant world. His outward life was full of proofs of the wide and deep benevolence of his nature; and it was only shallow minds who dwelt upon some petty defects of his character. The deep wisdom gained by contemplation comes forth whenever he talks of childhood. This subject always possesses inspiration for him, as when he says:—

> "Our birth is but a sleep and forgetting;
> The soul that rises with us, our life's star,
> Hath had elsewhere its setting,
> And cometh from afar.
> Not in entire forgetfulness,
> And not in utter nakedness,
> But trailing clouds of glory do we come
> From God who is our home.
> Heaven lies about us in our infancy!
> Shades of the prison-house begin to close
> Upon the growing boy,
> But he beholds the light, and whence it flows,—
> He sees it in his joy.
> The youth, who daily farther from the east
> Must travel, still is Nature's priest,
> And by the vision splendid
> Is on his way attended;
> At length the man perceives it die away,
> And fade into the light of common day."

This conception of the nearness of the child to the unseen made all children sacred in his eyes, and he always felt that he learned more from them than he could teach them. He expresses this thought often, as thus:—

> "Oh dearest, dearest boy; my heart
> For better lore would seldom yearn,

Could I but teach the hundredth part
Of what from thee I learn."

And again:—

"Dear child; dear girl; thou walkest with me here;
If thou appear untouched by solemn thought,
Thy nature is not therefore less divine;
Thou liest in Abraham's bosom all the year;
And worship'st at the Temple's inner shrine,
God being with thee when we know it not."

His own children he loved almost to idolatry, and after the lapse of forty years, would speak with the deepest emotion of the little ones who had died. Indeed, he was a man of profound feeling, passionate and intense in his loves, though outwardly calm and self-contained. He himself says:—

"Had I been a writer of love-poetry, it would have been natural for me to write it with a degree of warmth which could hardly have been approved by my principles, and which might have been undesirable for the reader."

His sister Dorothy frequently refers to the intensity of his passionate affection for the members of his family, and of the full and free expression he gave it. Greatly indeed have they erred who have imagined him as by nature cold or even tranquil. "What strange workings," writes one, "are there in his great mind! how fearfully strong are all his feelings and affections! If his intellect had been less powerful they would have destroyed him long ago." Indeed, no one who had ever known him well could doubt this intensity of nature, this smothered fire. It leaped out in bursts of anger at the report of evil doings; in long and violent tramps over the mountains, in exaggerated grief at the death of loved ones; and in almost unnatural intensity of devotion, to his sister first,

17

and his daughter Dora afterwards. It took the form of passionate adoration of Nature in his poems, and of passionate patriotism as well, and it gave strength and fire to the best of all his literary work.

Let us dwell for a moment more upon the married life of the poet,—that calm and quiet and happy life which made it possible that he should be the poet he was, unvexed by worldly cares or vanities. His late biographer, Mr. Myers, tells us:—

"The life which the young couple led was one of primitive simplicity. In some respects it was even less luxurious than that of the peasants about them. They drank water, and ate the simplest fare. Miss Wordsworth had long rendered existence possible for her brother, on the narrowest of means, by her unselfish energy and skill in household management; and plain living and high thinking were equally congenial to the new inmate of the frugal home. Wordsworth gardened; and all together, or oftenest the poet and his sister, wandered almost daily over the neighboring hills. Narrow means did not prevent them from offering a generous welcome to their few friends, especially Coleridge and his family, who repeatedly stayed for months under Wordsworth's roof. Miss Wordsworth's letters breathe the very spirit of hospitality in their naïve details of the little sacrifices gladly made for the sake of the presence of these honored guests. But for the most part the life was solitary and uneventful. Books they had few, neighbors none, and their dependence was almost entirely upon external nature."

The cottage in which they lived was very small, but they covered it with roses and honeysuckles, and had a little garden around it. Inside, all was the perfection of simplicity, but the soul of neatness and thrift pervaded everything, and love glorified it all.

They had a little boat upon the lake, and rowing and walking were their pleasures.

They lived in this simple fashion that the poet might pursue his high vocation, and not be put into the treadmill of any steady work. In after years, through bequests from friends and a pension from Government, they were made more prosperous, and their declining years were cheered by an assured abundance. Rydal Mount has been described so often that it is familiar to most readers. The house stands looking southward, on the rocky side of Nab Scar above Rydal Lake. The garden is terraced, and was full of flowering alleys in the poet's time. There was a tall ash-tree in which the thrushes always sung, and a laburnum in which the osier cage of the doves was hung. There were stone steps, in which poppies and wild geraniums filled the interstices; and rustic seats here and there, where they all sat all day during the pleasant weather. The poet spent very little time in-doors. He lived constantly in the open air, composing all his poems there, and committing them to paper afterwards. Their friends grew more numerous in later life, and Wordsworth much enjoyed their companionship, being himself very bright and delightful company when in the mood for talk. Here that strange being, Thomas De Quincey, came and lived, purposely to be near the poet. Coleridge was always at call, genial Kit North paid loyal court to the great man from the first, and loving and gentle Charles Lamb came at times, sadly missing the town, and almost afraid of the mountains. Here Dr. Arnold of Rugby came often from Fox How, his own house in the neighborhood; hither Harriet Martineau walked over from Ambleside, with some new theory of the universe to expound; and here poor Hartley Coleridge passed the happiest hours of his unfortunate life. Wordsworth's kindness and tenderness to this poor son of his great friend were well known to his little world, and show some of the most pleasing traits of his character. This amiable and gifted man, Hartley Coleridge, ruined himself through the weakness of his will, finding it utterly impossible to leave wine alone, even when he knew it was ruining his life, and so sorely afflicting his friends. Wordsworth dealt with him like a father, recognizing the weakness of his character, and perhaps being able to trace it to inherited tendencies,—the elder Coleridge's devotion to opium being well known. Poor Hartley lies with Wordsworth's own family in the little churchyard at Grasmere, and we trust in that quiet retreat sleeps well, at the foot of his friend and master.

Wordsworth's last years were of great solemnity and calm. He lived in retrospection, and dwelt much upon the unseen world. The deep spirituality of his nature was shown in all his later life. He was absorbed, as it were, in thoughts of God, and of the ultimate destiny of man. All worldly interests died out, and he was able to write even of his fame:—

"It is indeed a deep satisfaction to hope and believe
that my poetry will be, while it lasts, a help to the
cause of virtue and truth, especially among the young.
As for myself, it seems now of little moment how
long I may be remembered. When a man pushes
off in his little boat into the great seas of Infinity
and Eternity, it surely signifies little how long he
is kept in sight by watchers from the shore."

A CHAPTER FROM
Home Life of Great Authors, 1887

WM. WORDSWORTH.

By Elbert Hubbard

Even such a shell the universe itself
Is to the ear of Faith; and there are times,
I doubt not, when to you it doth impart
Authentic tidings of invisible things;
Of ebb and flow and ever-during power;
And central peace subsisting at the heart
Of endless agitation. Here you stand,
Adore and worship, when you know it not;
Pious beyond the intention of your thought;
Devout above the meaning of your will.

—WORDSWORTH

Some one has told us that Heaven is not a place but a condition of mind, and it is possible that he is right.

But if Heaven is a place, surely it is not unlike Grasmere. Such loveliness of landscape—such sylvan stretches of crystal water—peace and quiet and rest!

Great, green hills lift their heads to the skies, and all the old stone walls and hedgerows are covered with trailing vines and blooming flowers. The air is rich with song of birds, sweet with perfume, and the blossoms gaily shower their petals on the passer-by. Overhead, white, billowy clouds float lazily over their background of ethereal blue. Cool June breezes fan the cheek. Distant knolls are dotted with flocks of sheep whose bells tinkle dreamily; and drowsy hum of beetle makes the bass, while lark

21

song forms the air of the sweet symphony that Nature plays. Such was Grasmere as I first saw it.

To love the plain, homely, common, simple things of earth, of these to sing; to make the familiar beautiful and the commonplace enchanting; to cause each bush to burn with the actual presence of the living God: this is the poet's office. And if the poet lives near Grasmere, his task does not seem difficult.

From Seventeen Hundred Ninety-nine to Eighteen Hundred Eight, Wordsworth lived at Dove Cottage. Thanks to a few earnest souls, the place is now secured to the people of England and the lovers of poetry wherever they may be. A good old woman has charge of the cottage, and for a slight fee shows you the house and garden and little orchard and objects of interest, all the while talking: and you are glad, for, although unlettered, she is reverent and honest. She was born here, and all she knows is Wordsworth and the people and the things he loved. Is not this enough?

Here Wordsworth lived before anything he wrote was published in book form: here his best work was done, and here Dorothy—splendid, sympathetic Dorothy—-was inspiration, critic, friend. But who inspired Dorothy? Coleridge perhaps more than all others, and we know somewhat of their relationship as told in Dorothy's diary. There is a little Wordsworth Library in Dove Cottage, and I sat at the window of "De Quincey's room" and read for an hour. Says Dorothy:

"Sat until four o'clock reading dear Coleridge's letters."

"We paced the garden until moonrise at one o'clock—we three, brother, Coleridge and I." "I read Spenser to him aloud and then we had a midnight tea."

Here in this little, terraced garden, behind the stone cottage with its low ceilings and wide window-seats and little, diamond panes, she in her misery wrote:

"Oh, the pity of it all! Yet there is recompense; every sight reminds me of Coleridge, dear, dear fellow; of our walks and talks by day and night; of all the bright and witty, and sad sweet

22

things of which we spoke and read. I was melancholy and could not talk, and at last I eased my heart by weeping."

Alas, too often there is competition between brother and sister, then follow misunderstandings; but here the brotherly and sisterly love stands out clear and strong after these hundred years have passed, and we contemplate it with delight. Was ever woman more honestly and better praised than Dorothy?

> "The blessings of my later years
> Were with me when I was a boy.
> She gave me eyes, she gave me ears,
> And humble cares and gentle fears,
> A heart! the fountain of sweet tears,
> And love and thought and joy.
> And she hath smiles to earth unknown,
> Smiles that with motion of their own
> Do spread and sink and rise;
> That come and go with endless play,
> And ever as they pass away
> Are hidden in her eyes."

And so in a dozen or more poems, we see Dorothy reflected. She was the steel on which he tried his flint. Everything he wrote was read to her, then she read it alone, balancing the sentences in the delicate scales of her womanly judgment. "Heart of my heart, is this well done?" When she said, "This will do," it was no matter who said otherwise.

Back of the house on the rising hillside is the little garden. Hewn out of the solid rock is "Dorothy's seat." There I rested while Mrs. Dixon discoursed of poet lore, and told me of how, many times, Coleridge and Dorothy had sat in the same seat and watched the stars.

Then I drank from "the well," which is more properly a spring; the stones that curb it were placed in their present position by the hand that wrote "The Prelude." Above the garden is the orchard, where the green linnet still sings, for the birds never grow old.

There, too, are the circling swallows; and in a snug little alcove of the cottage you can read "The Butterfly" from a first edition; and then you can go sit in the orchard, white with blossoms, and see the butterflies that suggested the poem. And if your eye is good you can discover down by the lakeside the daffodils, and listen the while to the cuckoo call.

Then in the orchard you can see not only "the daisy," but many of them, and, if you wish, Mrs. Dixon will let you dig a bunch of the daisies to take back to America; and if you do, I hope that yours will prosper as have mine, and that Wordsworth's flowers, like Wordsworth's verse, will gladden your heart when the blue sky of your life threatens to be o'ercast with gray.

Here Southey came, and "Thalaber" was read aloud in this little garden. Here, too, came Clarkson, the man with a fine feminine carelessness, as Dorothy said. Charles Lloyd sat here and discoursed with William Calvert. Sir George Beaumont forgot his title and rapped often at the quaint, hinged door. An artist was Beaumont, but his best picture they say is not equal to the lines that Wordsworth wrote about it. Sir George was not only a gentleman according to law, but one in heart, for he was a friend, kind, gentle and generous. With such a friend Wordsworth was rich indeed. But perhaps the friends we have are only our other selves, and we get what we deserve.

We must not forget the kindly face of Humphry Davy, whose gracious playfulness was ever a charm to the Wordsworths. The safety-lamp was then only an unspoken word, and perhaps few foresaw the sweetness and light that these two men would yet give to earth.

Walter Scott and his wife came to Dove Cottage in Eighteen Hundred Five. He did not bring his title, for it, like Humphry Davy's, was as yet unpacked down in London town. They slept in the little cubby-hole of a room in the upper southwest corner. One can imagine Dorothy taking Sir Walter's shaving-water up to him in the morning; and the savory smell of breakfast as

Mistress Mary poured the tea, while England's future laureate served the toast and eggs: Mr. Scott eating everything in sight and talking a torrent the while about art and philosophy as he passed his cup back, to the consternation of the hostess, whose frugal ways were not used to such ravages of appetite. Of course she did not know that a combined novelist and rhymster ate twice as much as a simple poet.

Afterwards Mrs. Scott tucked up her dress, putting on one of Dorothy's aprons, and helped do the dishes.

Then Coleridge came over and they all climbed to the summit of Helm Crag. Shy little De Quincey had read some of Wordsworth's poems, and knew from their flavor that the man who penned them was a noble soul. He came to Grasmere to call on him: he walked past Dove Cottage twice, but his heart failed him and he went away unannounced. Later, he returned and found the occupants as simple folks as himself.

Happiness was there and good society; few books, but fine culture; plain living and high thinking.

Wordsworth lived at Rydal Mount for thirty-three years, yet the sweetest flowers of his life blossomed at Dove Cottage. For difficulty, toil, struggle, obscurity, poverty, mixed with aspiration and ambition—-all these were here. Success came later, but this is naught; for the achievement is more than the public acknowledgment of the deed.

After Wordsworth moved away, De Quincey rented Dove Cottage and lived in it for twenty-seven years. He acquired a library of more than five thousand volumes, making bookshelves on four sides of the little rooms from floor to ceiling. Some of these shelves still remain. Here he turned night into day and dreamed the dreams of "The Opium-Eater."

And all these are some of the things that Mrs. Dixon told me on that bright Summer day. What if I had heard them before! no difference. Dear old lady, I salute you and at your feet I lay my gratitude for a day of rare and quiet joy.

"Farewell, thou little nook of mountain ground,
Thou rocky corner in the lowest stair
Of that magnificent temple which does bound
One side of our whole vale with gardens rare,
Sweet garden-orchard, eminently fair,
The loveliest spot that man has ever found,
Farewell! We leave thee to Heaven's peaceful care,
Thee, and the Cottage which thou dost surround."

At places of pleasure and entertainment in the Far West, are often found functionaries known as "bouncers." It is the duty of the bouncer to give hints to objectionable visitors that their presence is not desired. And inasmuch as there are many men who can never take a hint without a kick, the bouncer is a person selected on account of his peculiar fitness—psychic and otherwise—for the place. We all have special talents, and these faculties should be used in a manner that will help our fellowmen on their way.

My acquaintanceship with the bouncer has been only general, not particular. Yet I have admired him from a distance, and the skill and eclat that he sometimes shows in a professional way has often excited my admiration.

In social usages, America borrows constantly from the mother country. But like all borrowing it seems to be one-sided, for seldom, very, very seldom, in point of etiquette and manners does England borrow from us. Yet there are exceptions.

It is a beautiful highway that skirts Lake Windermere and follows up through Ambleside. We get a glimpse of the old home of Harriet Martineau, and "Fox Howe," the home of Matthew Arnold. Just before Rydal Water is reached comes Rydal Road, running straight up the hillside, off from the turnpike. Rydal Mount is the third house up on the left-hand side, I knew the location, for I had read of it many times, and in my pocketbook I carried a picture taken from an old "Frank Leslie's," showing the house.

My heart beat fast as I climbed the hill. To visit the old home of one who was Poet Laureate of England is no small event in the life of a book-lover. I was full of poetry and murmured lines from "The Excursion" as I walked. Soon rare old Rydal Mount came in sight among the wealth of green. I stopped and sighed. Yes, yes, Wordsworth lived here for thirty-three years, and here he died; the spot whereon I then stood had been pressed many times by his feet. I walked slowly, with uncovered head, and approached the gate. It was locked. I fumbled at the latch; and just as there came a prospect of its opening, a loud, deep, guttural voice dashed over me like a wave:

"There—you! now, wot you want?"

The owner of this voice was not ten feet away, but he was standing up close to the wall and I had not seen him. I was somewhat startled at first. The man did not move. I stepped to one side to get a better view of my interlocutor, and saw him to be a large, red man of perhaps fifty. A handkerchief was knotted around his thick neck, and he held a heavy hoe in his hand. A genuine beefeater he was, only he ate too much beef and the ale he drank was evidently Extra XXX.

His scowl was so needlessly severe and his manner so belligerent that I—thrice armed, knowing my cause was just—could not restrain a smile. I touched my hat and said, "Ah, excuse me, Mr. Falstaff, you are the bouncer?"

"Never mind wot I am, sir—'oo are you?"

"I am a great admirer of Wordsworth——"

"That's the way they all begins. Cawn't ye hadmire 'im on that side of the wall as well as this?"

There is no use of wasting argument with a man of this stamp; besides that, his question was to the point. But there are several ways of overcoming one's adversary: I began feeling in my pocket for pence. My enemy ceased glaring, stepped up to the locked gate as though he half-wished to be friendly, and there was sorrow in his voice: "Don't tempt me, sir; don't do ut! The Missus is peekin' out of the shutters at us now."

"And do you never admit visitors, even to the grounds?"

"No, sir, never, God 'elp me! and there's many an honest bob I could turn by ut, and no one 'urt. But I've lost my place twic't by ut. They took me back though. The Guv'ner 'ud never forgive me again. 'It's three times and out, Mister 'Opkins,' says 'ee, only last Whitsuntide."

"But visitors do come?"

"Yes, sir; but they never gets in. Mostly 'mer'cans; they don't know no better, sir. They picks all the ivy orf the outside of the wall, and you sees yourself there's no leaves on the lower branches of that tree. Then they carries away so many pebbles from out there that I've to dump in a fresh weelbarrel full o' gravel every week, sir, don't you know."

He thrust a pudgy, freckled hand through the bars of the gate to show that he bore me no ill-will, and also, I suppose, to mollify my disappointment. For although I had come too late to see the great poet himself and had even failed to see the inside of his house, yet I had at least been greeted at the gate by his proxy. I pressed the hand firmly, pocketed a handful of gravel as a memento, then turned and went my way.

And all there is to tell about my visit to Rydal Mount is this interview with the bouncer.

Wordsworth lived eighty years. His habitation, except for short periods, was never more than a few miles from his birthplace. His education was not extensive, his learning not profound. He lacked humor and passion; in his character there was little personal magnetism, and in his work there is small dramatic power.

He traveled more or less and knew humanity, but he did not know man. His experience in so-called practical things was slight, his judgment not accurate. So he lived—quietly, modestly, dreamily.

His dust rests in a country churchyard, the grave marked by a simple slab. A gnarled, old yew-tree stands guard above the grass-grown mound. The nearest railroad is fifteen miles away.

As a poet, Wordsworth stands in the front rank of the second class. Shelley, Browning, Mrs. Browning, Tennyson, far surpass him; and the sweet singer of Michigan, even in uninspired moments, never "threw off" anything worse than this:

> "And he is lean and he is sick:
> His body, dwindled and awry,
> Rests upon ankles swollen and thick;
> His legs are thin and dry.
> One prop he has, and only one,
> His wife, an aged woman,
> Lives with him near the waterfall,
> Upon the village common."

Jove may nod, but when he makes a move it counts.

Yet the influence of Wordsworth upon the thought and feeling of the world has been very great. He himself said, "The young will read my poems and be better for their truth." Many of his lines pass as current coin: "The child is father of the man," "The light that never was on land nor sea," "Not too bright and good for human nature's daily food," "Thoughts that do lie too deep for tears," "The mighty stream of tendency," and many others. "Plain living and high thinking" is generally given to Emerson, but he discovered it in Wordsworth, and recognizing it as his own he took it. In a certain book of quotations, "The still sad music of humanity" is given to Shakespeare; but to equalize matters we sometimes attribute to Wordsworth "The Old Oaken Bucket."

The men who win those who correct an abuse. Wordsworth's work was a protest—mild yet firm—against the bombastic and artificial school of the Eighteenth Century. Before his day the "timber" used by poets consisted of angels, devils, ghosts, gods; onslaught, tourneys, jousts, tempests of hate and torrents of wrath, always of course with a very beautiful and very susceptible young lady just around the corner. The women in those days were always young and ever beautiful, but seldom wise and not often good. The men were saints or else "bad," generally bad. Like the cats of Kilkenny, they fought on slight cause.

Our young man at Hawkshead School saw this: it pleased him not, and he made a list of the things on which he would write poems. This list includes: sunset, moonrise, starlight, mist, brooks, shells, stones, butterflies, moths, swallows, linnets, thrushes, wagoners, babies, bark of trees, leaves, nests, fishes, rushes, leeches, cobwebs, clouds, deer, music, shade, swans, crags and snow. He kept his vow and "went it one better," for among his verses I find the following titles: "Lines Left Upon a Seat in a Yew-Tree," "Lines Composed a Few Miles Above Tintern Abbey," "To a Wounded Butterfly," "To Dora's Portrait," "To the Cuckoo," "On Seeing a Needlebook Made in the Shape of a Harp," etc.

Wordsworth's service to humanity consists in the fact that he has shown us old truth in a new light, and has made plain the close relationship that exists between physical nature and the soul of man. Is this much or little? I think it is much. When we realize that we are a part of all that we see, or hear, or feel, we are not lonely. But to feel a sense of separation is to feel the chill of death.

Wordsworth taught that the earth is the universal Mother and that the life of the flower has its source in the same universal life from whence ours is derived. To know this truth is to feel a tenderness, a kindliness, a spirit of fraternalism, toward every manifestation of this universal life. No attempt was made to say the last word, only a wish to express the truth that the spirit of God is manifest on every hand.

Now this is a very simple philosophy. No far-reaching, syllogistic logic is required to prove it; no miracle, nor special dispensation is needed; you just feel that it is so, that's all, and it gives you peace. Children, foolish folks, old men, whose sands of life are nearly run, comprehend it. But heaven bless you! you can't prove any such foolishness. Jeffrey saw the ridiculousness of these assumptions and so he declared, "This will never do," and for twenty years "The Edinburgh Review" never ceased to fling off fleers and jeers—and to criticize and scoff. That a great periodical, rich and influential, in the city which was the very center of learning, should go so much out of its way to attack a quiet countryman living in a four-roomed cottage, away off in the hills of Cumberland, seems a little queer.

Then, this countryman did not seek to found a kingdom, nor to revolutionize society, nor did he force upon the world his pattypan rhymes about linnets, and larks, and daffodils. Far from it: he was very modest—diffident, in fact—and his song was quite in the minor key, but still the chain-shot and bombs of literary warfare were sent hissing in his direction.

There is a little story about a certain general who figured as division-commander in the War of Secession: this warrior had his headquarters, for a time, in a typical Southern home in the Tennessee Mountains. The house had a large fireplace and chimney; in this chimney, swallows had nests. One day, as the great man was busy at his maps, working out a plan of campaign against the enemy, the swallows made quite an uproar. Perhaps some of the eggs were hatching; anyway, the birds were needlessly noisy in their domestic affairs, and it disturbed the great man—he grew nervous. He called his adjutant. "Sir," said the mighty warrior, "dislodge those damn pests in the chimney, without delay."

Two soldiers were ordered to climb the roof and dislodge the enemy. Yet the swallows were not dislodged, for the soldiers could not reach them.

So Jeffrey's tirades were unavailing, and Wordsworth was not dislodged.

"He might as well try to crush Skiddaw," said Southey.

A Chapter from
Little Journeys to the Homes of the Great,1894

WORDSWORTH'S POETRY.

DELIVERED
EXTEMPORE AT MANCHESTER.

By George Macdonald

The history of the poetry of Wordsworth is a true reflex of the man himself. The life of Wordsworth was not outwardly eventful, but his inner life was full of conflict, discovery, and progress. His outward life seems to have been so ordered by Providence as to favour the development of the poetic life within. Educated in the country, and spending most of his life in the society of nature, he was not subjected to those violent external changes which have been the lot of some poets. Perfectly fitted as he was to cope with the world, and to fight his way to any desired position, he chose to retire from it, and in solitude to work out what appeared to him to be the true destiny of his life.

The very element in which the mind of Wordsworth lived and moved was a Christian pantheism. Allow me to explain the word. The poets of the Old Testament speak of everything as being the work of God's hand:—We are the "work of his hand;" "The world was made by him." But in the New Testament there is a higher form used to express the relation in which we stand to him—"We are his offspring;" not the work of his hand, but the children that came forth from his heart. Our own poet Goldsmith, with the high instinct of genius, speaks of God as having "loved us into being." Now I think this is not only true with regard to man, but true likewise with regard to the world in which we live. This world is not merely a thing which God hath made, subjecting it to laws; but it is an expression of the thought, the feeling, the heart of God himself. And so it must be; because, if man be the child of God, would he not feel to be out of his element if he lived in a world which came, not from the heart of God, but only from his hand? This Christian pantheism, this belief that God is in everything, and showing himself in everything, has been much brought to the light by the poets of the past generation, and has its influence still, I hope, upon the poets of the present. We are not satisfied that the world should be a proof and varying indication of the intellect of God. That was how Paley viewed it. He taught us to believe there is a God from the mechanism of the world. But, allowing all the argument to be quite correct, what does it prove? A mechanical God, and nothing more.

Let us go further; and, looking at beauty, believe that God is the first of artists; that he has put beauty into nature, knowing how it will affect us, and intending that it should so affect us; that he has embodied his own grand thoughts thus that we might see them and be glad. Then, let us go further still, and believe that whatever we feel in the highest moments of truth shining through beauty, whatever comes to our souls as a power of life, is meant to be seen and felt by us, and to be regarded not as the work of his hand, but as the flowing forth of his heart, the flowing forth of his love of us, making us blessed in the union of his heart and ours.

Now, Wordsworth is the high priest of nature thus regarded. He saw God present everywhere; not always immediately, in his own form, it is true; but whether he looked upon the awful mountain-peak, sky-encompassed with loveliness, or upon the face of a little child, which is as it were eyes in the face of nature—in all things he felt the solemn presence of the Divine Spirit. By Keats this presence was recognized only as the spirit of beauty; to Wordsworth, God, as the Spirit of Truth, was manifested through the forms of the external world.

I have said that the life of Wordsworth was so ordered as to bring this out of him, in the forms of *his* art, to the ears of men. In childhood even his conscience was partly developed through the influences of nature upon him. He thus retrospectively describes this special influence of nature:—

One summer evening (led by her) I found
A little boat, tied to a willow tree,
Within a rocky cave, its usual home.
Straight I unloosed her chain, and stepping in,
Pushed from the shore. It was an act of stealth,
And troubled pleasure, nor without the voice
Of mountain echoes did my boat move on,
Leaving behind her still, on either side,
Small circles glittering idly in the moon,
Until they melted all into one track
Of sparkling light. But now, like one who rows
Proud of his skill, to reach a chosen point
With an unswerving line, I fixed my view
Upon the summit of a craggy ridge,
The horizon's utmost boundary; far above
Was nothing but the stars and the grey sky.
She was an elfin pinnace; lustily
I dipped my oars into the silent lake,
And, as I rose upon the stroke, my boat
Went heaving through the water like a swan;
When, from behind that craggy steep, till then
The horizon's bound, a huge peak, black and huge,
As if with voluntary power instinct,
Upreared its head. I struck and struck again,
And, growing still in stature, the grim shape
Towered up between me and the stars, and still
For so it seemed, with purpose of its own,
And measured motion like a living thing,
Strode after me. With trembling oars I turned,

And through the silent water stole my way
Back to the covert of the willow tree;
There in her mooring place I left my bark,
And through the meadows homeward went, in grave
And serious mood; but after I had seen
That spectacle, for many days, my brain
Worked with a dim and undetermined sense
Of unknown modes of being; o'er my thoughts
There hung a darkness, call it solitude,
Or blank desertion. No familiar shapes
Remained, no pleasant images of trees,
Of sea, or sky, no colours of green fields;
But huge and mighty forms, that do not live
Like living men, moved slowly through the mind
By day, and were a trouble to my dreams.

Here we see that a fresh impulse was given to his life even in boyhood, by the influence of nature. If we have had any similar experience, we shall be able to enter into this feeling of Wordsworth's; if not, the tale will be almost incredible.

One passage more I would refer to, as showing what Wordsworth felt with regard to nature, in his youth; and the growth that took place in him in consequence. Nature laid up in the storehouse of his mind and heart her most beautiful and grand forms, whence they might be brought, afterwards, to be put to the highest human service. I quote only a few lines from that poem, deservedly a favourite with all the lovers of Wordsworth, "Lines written above Tintern Abbey:"—

I cannot paint
What then I was. The sounding cataract
Haunted me like a passion; the tall rock,
The mountain, and the deep and gloomy wood,
Their colours and their forms, were then to me
An appetite; a feeling and a love,

35

That had no need of a remoter charm
By thought supplied, nor any interest
Unborrowed from the eye.—That time is past,
And all its aching joys are now no more,
And all its dizzy raptures. Not for this
Faint I, nor mourn nor murmur; other gifts
Have followed; for such loss, I would believe,
Abundant recompense. For I have learned
To look on nature, not as in the hour
Of thoughtless youth; but hearing oftentimes
The still, sad music of humanity,
Nor harsh, nor grating, though of ample power
To chasten and subdue. And I have felt
A presence that disturbs me with the joy
Of elevated thoughts; a sense sublime
Of something far more deeply interfused,
Whose dwelling is the light of setting suns,
And the round ocean, and the living air
And the blue sky, and in the mind of man;
A motion and a spirit, that impels
All thinking things, all objects of all thought,
And rolls through all things.

In this little passage you see the growth of the influence of nature on the mind of the poet. You observe, too, that nature passes into poetry; that form is sublimed into speech. You see the result of the conjunction of the mind of man, and the mind of God manifested in His works; spirit coming to know the speech of spirit. The outflowing of spirit in nature is received by the poet, and he utters again, in his form, what God has already uttered in His. Wordsworth wished to give to man what he found in nature. It was to him a power of good, a world of teaching, a strength of life. He knew that nature was not his, and that his enjoyment of nature was given to him that he might give it to man. It was the birthright of man.

36

But what did Wordsworth find in nature? To begin with the lowest; he found amusement in nature. Right amusement is a part of teaching; it is the childish form of teaching, and if we can get this in nature, we get something that lies near the root of good. In proof that Wordsworth found this, I refer to a poem which you probably know well, "The Daisy." The poet sits playing with the flower, and listening to the suggestions that come to him of odd resemblances that this flower bears to other things. He likens the daisy to—

> A little cyclops, with one eye
> Staring to threaten and defy,
> That thought comes next—and instantly
> The freak is over,
> The shape will vanish—and behold
> A silver shield with boss of gold,
> That spreads itself, some faëry bold
> In fight to cover!

Look at the last stanza, too, and you will see how close amusement may lie to deep and earnest thought:—

> Bright Flower! for by that name at last
> When all my reveries are past,
> I call thee, and to that cleave fast,
>   Sweet silent creature!
> That breath'st with me in sun and air,
> Do thou, as thou art wont, repair
> My heart with gladness, and a share
>   Of thy meek nature!

But Wordsworth found also joy in nature, which is a better thing than amusement, and consequently easier to be found. We can often have joy where we can have no amusement,—

I wandered lonely as a cloud
    That floats on high o'er vales and hills
When all at once I saw a crowd,
    A host, of golden daffodils;
Beside the lake, beneath the trees,
Fluttering and dancing in the breeze.
The waves beside them danced; but they
    Out-did the sparkling waves in glee:
A poet could not but be gay,
    In such a jocund company:
I gazed—and gazed—but little thought
What Health the show to me had brought.

"For oft, when on my couch I lie
    In vacant or in pensive mood,
They flash upon that inward eye
    Which is the bliss of solitude;
And then my heart with pleasure fills,
And dances with the daffodils."

This is the joy of the eye, as far as that can be separated from the joy of the whole nature; for his whole nature rejoiced in the joy of the eye; but it was simply joy; there was no further teaching, no attempt to go through this beauty and find the truth below it. We are not always to be in that hungry, restless condition, even after truth itself. If we keep our minds quiet and ready to receive truth, and *sometimes* are hungry for it, that is enough.

Going a step higher, you will find that he sometimes *draws* a lesson from nature, seeming almost to force a meaning from her. I do not object to this, if he does not make too much of it as *existing* in nature. It is rather finding a meaning in nature that he brought to it. The meaning exists, if not *there*. For illustration I refer to another poem. Observe that Wordsworth found the lesson because he looked for it, and *would* find it.

38

This Lawn, a carpet all alive
With shadows flung from leaves—to strive
    In dance, amid a press
Of sunshine, an apt emblem yields
Of Worldlings revelling in the fields
    Of strenuous idleness.
Yet, spite of all this eager strife,
This ceaseless play, the genuine life
    That serves the steadfast hours,
Is in the grass beneath, that grows
Unheeded, and the mute repose
    Of sweetly-breathing flowers.

Whether he forced this lesson from nature, or not, it is a good lesson, teaching a great many things with regard to life and work.

Again, nature sometimes flashes a lesson on his mind; *gives* it to him—and when nature gives, we cannot but receive. As in this sonnet composed during a storm,—

One who was suffering tumult in his soul
Yet failed to seek the sure relief of prayer,
Went forth; his course surrendering to the care
Of the fierce wind, while mid-day lightnings prowl
Insiduously, untimely thunders growl;
While trees, dim-seen, in frenzied numbers tear
The lingering remnant of their yellow hair,
And shivering wolves, surprised with darkness, howl
As if the sun were not. He raised his eye
Soul-smitten; for, that instant, did appear
Large space (mid dreadful clouds) of purest sky,
An azure disc—shield of Tranquillity;
Invisible, unlooked-for, minister
Of providential goodness ever nigh!

Observe that he was not looking for this; he had not thought of praying; he was in such distress that it had benumbed the outgoings of his spirit towards the source whence alone sure comfort comes. He went out into the storm; and the uproar in the outer world was in harmony with the tumult within his soul. Suddenly a clear space in the sky makes him feel—he has no time to think about it—that there is a shield of tranquillity spread over him. For was it not as it were an opening up into that region where there are no storms; the regions of peace, because the regions of love, and truth, and purity,—the home of God himself?

There is yet a higher and more sustained influence exercised by nature, and that takes effect when she puts a man into that mood or condition in which thoughts come of themselves. That is perhaps the best thing that can be done for us, the best at least that nature can do. It is certainly higher than mere intellectual teaching. That nature did this for Wordsworth is very clear; and it is easily intelligible. If the world proceeded from the imagination of God, and man proceeded from the love of God, it is easy to believe that that which proceeded from the imagination of God should rouse the best thoughts in the mind of a being who proceeded from the love of God. This I think is the relation between man and the world. As an instance of what I mean, I refer to one of Wordsworth's finest poems, which he classes under the head of "Evening Voluntaries." It was composed upon an evening of extraordinary splendour and beauty:—

"Had this effulgence disappeared
With flying haste, I might have sent,
Among the speechless clouds, a look
Of blank astonishment;
But 'tis endued with power to stay,
And sanctify one closing day,
That frail Mortality may see—
What is?—ah no, but what can, be!

Time was when field and watery cove
With modulated echoes rang,
While choirs of fervent Angels sang
Their vespers in the grove;
Or, crowning, star-like, each some sovereign height,
Warbled, for heaven above and earth below,
Strains suitable to both. Such holy rite,
Methinks, if audibly repeated now
From hill or valley, could not move
Sublimer transport, purer love,
Than doth this silent spectacle—the gleam—
The shadow—and the peace supreme!
"No sound is uttered,—but a deep
And solemn harmony pervades
The hollow vale from steep to steep,
And penetrates the glades.
"Wings at my shoulders seem to play;
But, rooted here, I stand and gaze
On those bright steps that heaven-ward raise
Their practicable way.
Come forth, ye drooping old men, look abroad,
And see to what fair countries ye are bound!
"Dread Power! whom peace and calmness serve
No less than Nature's threatening voice,
From THEE, if I would swerve,
Oh, let Thy grace remind me of the light
Full early lost, and fruitlessly deplored;
Which, at this moment, on my waking sight
Appears to shine, by miracle restored;
My soul, though yet confined to earth,
Rejoices in a second birth!"

Picture the scene for yourselves; and observe how it moves in
him the sense of responsibility, and the prayer, that if he has in
any matter wandered from the right road, if he has forgotten the

simplicity of childhood in the toil of life, he may, from this time, remember the vow that he now records—from this time to press on towards the things that are unseen, but which are manifested through the things that are seen. I refer you likewise to the poem "Resolution and Independence," commonly called "The Leech Gatherer;" also to that grandest ode that has ever been written, the "Ode on Immortality." You will find there, whatever you may think of his theory, in the latter, sufficient proof that nature was to him a divine teaching power. Do not suppose that I mean that man can do without more teaching than nature's, or that a man with only nature's teaching would have seen these things in nature. No, the soul must be tuned to such things. Wordsworth could not have found such things, had he not known something that was more definite and helpful to him; but this known, then nature was full of teaching. When we understand the Word of God, then we understand the works of God; when we know the nature of an artist, we know his pictures; when we have known and talked with the poet, we understand his poetry far better. To the man of God, all nature will be but changeful reflections of the face of God.

Loving man as Wordsworth did, he was most anxious to give him this teaching. How was he to do it? By poetry. Nature put into the crucible of a loving heart becomes poetry. We cannot explain poetry scientifically; because poetry is something beyond science. The poet may be man of science, and the man of science may be a poet; but poetry includes science, and the man who will advance science most, is the man who, other qualifications being equal, has most of the poetic faculty in him. Wordsworth defines poetry to be "the impassioned expression which is on the face of science." Science has to do with the construction of things. The casting of the granite ribs of the mighty earth, and all the thousand operations that result in the manifestations on its surface, this is the domain of science. But when there come the grass-bearing meadows, the heaven-reared hills, the great streams that go ever downward, the bubbling fountains that ever arise, the wind that wanders amongst the leaves, and the odours that are wafted upon its wings; when we have colour, and shape, and sound, then we have the material with which poetry has to do. Science has to do with the underwork. For what does this great central world exist, with its hidden winds and waters, its upheavings and its downsinkings, its strong frame of rock, and its heart of fire? What do they all exist for? Not for themselves surely, but for the sake of this out-spreading world of beauty, that floats up, as it were, to the surface of the shapeless region of force. Science has to do with the one, and poetry with the other: poetry is "the impassioned expression that is on the face of science." To illustrate it still further. You are walking in the woods, and you find the first primrose of the year. You feel almost as if you had found a child. You know in yourself that you have found a new beauty and a new joy, though you have seen it a thousand times before. It is a primrose. A little flower that looks at me, thinks itself into my heart, and gives me a pleasure distinct in itself, and which I feel as if I could not do without. The impassioned expression on the face of this little outspread flower is its childhood; it means trust, consciousness of protection, faith, and hope. Science, in the person of the botanist, comes after you, and pulls it to pieces to see its construction, and delights the intellect; but the science itself is dead, and kills what it touches. The flower exists not for it, but for the expression on its face, which is its poetry,—that expression which you feel to mean a living thing; that expression which makes you feel that this flower is, as it were, just growing out of the heart of God. The intellect itself is but the scaffolding for the uprearing of the spiritual nature.

It will make all this yet plainer, if you can suppose a human form to be created without a soul in it. Divine science *has* put it together, but only for the sake of the outshining soul that shall cause it to live, and move, and have a being of its own in God. When you see the face lighted up with soul, when you recognize in it thought and feeling, joy and love, then you know that here is the end for which it was made. Thus you see the relation that poetry has to science; and you find that, to speak in an apparent paradox, the surface is the deepest after all; for, through the surface, for the sake of which all this building went on, we have, as it were, a window into the depths of truth. There is not a form that lives in the world, but is a window cloven through the blank darkness of nothingness, to let us look into the heart, and feeling, and nature of God. So the surface of things is the best and the deepest, provided it is not mere surface, but the impassioned expression, for the sake of which the science of God has thought and laboured.

Satisfied that this was the nature of poetry, and wanting to convey this to the minds of his fellow-men, "What vehicle," Wordsworth may be supposed to have asked himself, "shall I use? How shall I decide what form of words to employ? Where am I to find the right language for speaking such great things to men?" He saw that the poetry of the eighteenth century (he was born in 1770) was not like nature at all, but was an artificial thing, with no more originality in it than there would be in a picture a hundred times copied, the copyists never reverting to the original.

You cannot look into this eighteenth century poetry, excepting, of course, a great proportion of the poetry of Cowper and Thompson, without being struck with the sort of agreement that nothing should be said naturally. A certain set form and mode was employed for saying things that ought never to have been said twice in the same way. Wordsworth resolved to go back to the root of the thing, to the natural simplicity of speech; he would have none of these stereotyped forms of expression. "Where shall I find," said he, "the language that will be simple and powerful?" And he came to the conclusion that the language of the common people was the only language suitable for his purpose.

Your experience of the everyday language of the common people may be that it is not poetical. True, but not even a poet can speak poetically in his stupid moments. Wordsworth's idea was to take the language of the common people in their uncommon moods, in their high and, consequently, simple moods, when their minds are influenced by grief, hope, reverence, worship, love; for then he believed he could get just the language suitable for the poet. As far as that language will go, I think he was right, if I may venture to give an opinion in support of Wordsworth. Of course, there will occur necessities to the poet which would not be comprehended in the language of a man whose thoughts had never moved in the same directions, but the kind of language will be the right thing, and I have heard such amongst the common people myself—language which they did not know to be poetic, but which fell upon my ear and heart as profoundly poetic both in its feeling and its form.

In attempting to carry out this theory, I am not prepared to say that Wordsworth never transgressed his own self-imposed laws. But he adhered to his theory to the last.

A friend of the poet's told me that Wordsworth had to him expressed his belief that he would be remembered longest, not by his sonnets, as his friend thought, but by his lyrical ballads, those for which he had been reviled and laughed at; the most by critics who could not understand him, and who were unworthy to read what he had written. As a proof of this let me read to you three verses, composing a poem that was especially marked for derision:—

> She dwelt among the untrodden ways,
> Beside the springs of Dove;
> A maid whom there were none to praise,
> And very few to love.
> A violet by a mossy stone.
> Half hidden from the eye;
> Fair as a star, when only one
> Is shining in the sky.
> She lived unknown, and few could know

When Lucy ceased to be;
But she is in her grave, and Oh!
The difference to me.

The last line was especially chosen as the object of ridicule; but I think with most of us the feeling will be, that its very simplicity of expression is overflowing in suggestion, it throws us back upon our own experience; for, instead of trying to utter what he felt, he says in those simple and common words, "You who have known anything of the kind, will know what the difference to me is, and only you can know." "My intention and desire," he says in one of his essays, "are that the interest of the poem shall owe nothing to the circumstances; but that the circumstances shall be made interesting by the thing itself." In most novels, for instance, the attempt is made to interest us in worthless, commonplace people, whom, if we had our choice, we would far rather not meet at all, by surrounding them with peculiar and extraordinary circumstances; but this is a low source of interest. Wordsworth was determined to owe nothing to such an adventitious cause. For illustration allow me to read that well-known little ballad, "The Reverie of Poor Susan," and you will see how entirely it bears out what he lays down as his theory. The scene is in London:—

At the corner of Wood-street, when daylight appears,
Hangs a Thrush that sings loud, it
    has sung for three years;
Poor Susan has passed by the spot, and has heard,
In the silence of morning, the song of the Bird.
'Tis a note of enchantment: what ails her? She sees
A mountain ascending, a vision of trees;
Bright volumes of vapour through Lothbury glide,
And a river flows on through the vale of Cheapside.
Green pastures she views in the midst of the dale,
Down which she so often has tripped with her pail;

And a single small cottage, a nest like a dove's,
The one only dwelling on earth that she loves.
She looks, and her heart is in heaven: but they fade,
The mist and the river, the hill and the shade:
The stream will not flow, and the hill will not rise,
And the colours have all passed away from her eyes!

Is any of the interest here owing to the circumstances? Is it not a very common incident? But has he not treated it so that it is not *commonplace* in the least? We recognize in this girl just the feelings we discover in ourselves, and acknowledge almost with tears her sisterhood to us all.

I have tried to make you feel something of what Wordsworth attempts to do, but I have not given you the best of his poems. Allow me to finish by reading the closing portion of the *Prelude*, the poem that was published after his death. It is addressed to Coleridge:—

Oh! yet a few short years of useful life,
And all will be complete, thy race be run,
Thy monument of glory will be raised;
Then, though (too weak to head the ways of truth)
This age fall back to old idolatry,
Though men return to servitude as fast
As the tide ebbs, to ignominy and shame
By nations sink together, we shall still
Find solace—knowing what we have learnt to know—
Rich in true happiness, if allowed to be
Faithful alike in forwarding a day
Of firmer trust, joint labourers in the work
(Should Providence such grace to us vouchsafe)
Of their deliverance, surely yet to come.
Prophets of Nature, we to them will speak
A lasting inspiration, sanctified
By reason, blest by faith: what we have loved,

Others will love, and we will teach them how;
Instruct them how the mind of man becomes
A thousand times more beautiful than the earth
On which he dwells, above this frame of things
(Which, 'mid all revolution in the hopes
And fears of men, doth still remain unchanged)
In beauty exalted, as it is itself
Of quality and fabric more divine.

A CHAPTER FROM
A Dish of Orts, 1893

IN WORDSWORTH'S COUNTRY.

By John Burroughs

No other English poet had touched me quite so closely as Wordsworth. All cultivated men delight in Shakespeare; he is the universal genius; but Wordsworth's poetry has more the character of a message, and a message special and personal, to a comparatively small circle of readers. He stands for a particular phase of human thought and experience, and his service to certain minds is like an initiation into a new order of truths. Note what a revelation he was to the logical mind of John Stuart Mill. His limitations make him all the more private and precious, like the seclusion of one of his mountain dales. He is not and can never be the world's poet, but more especially the poet of those who love solitude and solitary communion with nature. Shakespeare's attitude toward nature is for the most part like that of a gay, careless reveler, who leaves his companions for a moment to pluck a flower or gather a shell here and there, as they stroll

"By paved fountain, or by rushy brook,
Or on the beachéd margent of the sea."

He is, of course, preëminent in all purely poetic achievements, but his poems can never minister to the spirit in the way Wordsworth's do.

One can hardly appreciate the extent to which the latter poet has absorbed and reproduced the spirit of the Westmoreland scenery until he has visited that region. I paused there a few days

49

in early June, on my way south, and again on my return late in July. I walked up from Windermere to Grasmere, where, on the second visit, I took up my abode at the historic Swan Inn, where Scott used to go surreptitiously to get his mug of beer when he was stopping with Wordsworth.

The call of the cuckoo came to me from over Rydal Water as I passed along. I plucked my first foxglove by the roadside; paused and listened to the voice of the mountain torrent; heard

"The cataracts blow their trumpets from the steep;"

caught many a glimpse of green, unpeopled hills, urn-shaped dells, treeless heights, rocky promontories, secluded valleys, and clear, swift-running streams. The scenery was sombre; there were but two colors, green and brown, verging on black; wherever the rock cropped out of the green turf on the mountain-sides, or in the vale, it showed a dark face. But the tenderness and freshness of the green tints were something to remember,—the hue of the first springing April grass, massed and widespread in midsummer.

Then there was a quiet splendor, almost grandeur, about Grasmere vale, such as I had not seen elsewhere,—a kind of monumental beauty and dignity that agreed well with one's conception of the loftier strains of its poet. It is not too much dominated by the mountains, though shut in on all sides by them; that stately level floor of the valley keeps them back and defines them, and they rise from its outer margin like rugged, green-tufted, and green-draped walls.

It is doubtless this feature, as De Quincey says, this floor-like character of the valley, that makes the scenery of Grasmere more impressive than the scenery in North Wales, where the physiognomy of the mountains is essentially the same, but where the valleys are more bowl-shaped. Amid so much that is steep and rugged and broken, the eye delights in the repose and equilibrium of horizontal lines,—a bit of table-land, the surface of the lake, or the level of the valley bottom. The principal valleys of our own Catskill region all have this stately floor, so characteristic of Wordsworth's country. It was a pleasure which I daily indulged in to stand on the bridge by Grasmere Church, with that full, limpid stream before me, pausing and deepening under the stone embankment near where the dust of the poet lies, and let the eye sweep across the plain to the foot of the near mountains, or dwell upon their encircling summits above the tops of the trees and the roofs of the village. The water-ouzel loved to linger there, too, and would sit in contemplative mood on the stones around which the water loitered and murmured, its clear white breast alone defining it from the object upon which it rested. Then it would trip along the margin of the pool, or flit a few feet over its surface, and suddenly, as if it had burst like a bubble, vanish before my eyes; there would be a little splash of the water beneath where I saw it, as if the drop of which it was composed had reunited with the surface there. Then, in a moment or two, it would emerge from the water and take up its stand as dry and unruffled as ever. It was always amusing to see this plump little bird, so unlike a water-fowl in shape and manner, disappear in the stream. It did not seem to dive, but simply dropped into the water, as if its wings had suddenly failed it. Sometimes it fairly tumbled in from its perch. It was gone from sight in a twinkling, and, while you were wondering how it could accomplish the feat of walking on the bottom of the stream under there, it reappeared as unconcerned as possible. It is a song-bird, a thrush, and gives a feature to these mountain streams and waterfalls which ours, except on the Pacific coast, entirely lack. The stream that winds through Grasmere vale, and flows against the embankment of the churchyard, as the Avon at Stratford, is of great beauty,—clean, bright, full, trouty, with just a tinge of gypsy blood in its veins, which it gets from the black tarns on the mountains, and which adds to its richness of color. I saw an angler take a few trout from it, in a meadow near the village. After a heavy rain the stream was not roily, but slightly darker in hue; these fields and mountains are so turf-bound that no particle of soil is carried away by the water.

Falls and cascades are a great feature all through this country, as they are a marked feature in Wordsworth's poetry. One's ear is everywhere haunted by the sound of falling water; and, when the ear cannot hear them, the eye can see the streaks or patches of white foam down the green declivities. There are no trees above the valley bottom to obstruct the view, and no hum of woods to muffle the sounds of distant streams. When I was at Grasmere there was much rain, and this stanza of the poet came to mind:—

> "Loud is the Vale! The voice is up
> With which she speaks when storms are gone,
> A mighty unison of streams!
> Of all her voices, one!"

The words "vale" and "dell" come to have a new meaning after one has visited Wordsworth's country, just as the words "cottage" and "shepherd" also have so much more significance there and in Scotland than at home.

> "Dear child of Nature, let them rail!
> —There is a nest in a green dale,
> A harbor and a hold,
> Where thou, a wife and friend, shalt see
> Thy own delightful days, and be
> A light to young and old."

Every humble dwelling looks like a nest; that in which the poet himself lived had a cozy, nest-like look; and every vale is green,—a cradle amid rocky heights, padded and carpeted with the thickest turf.

Wordsworth is described as the poet of nature. He is more the poet of man, deeply wrought upon by a certain phase of nature,—the nature of those sombre, quiet, green, far-reaching mountain solitudes. There is a shepherd quality about him; he loves the flocks, the heights, the tarn, the tender herbage, the sheltered dell, the fold, with a kind of poetized shepherd instinct. Lambs and sheep and their haunts, and those who tend them, recur perpetually in his poems. How well his verse harmonizes with those high, green, and gray solitudes, where the silence is broken only by the bleat of lambs or sheep, or just stirred by the voice of distant waterfalls! Simple, elemental yet profoundly tender and human, he had

> "The primal sympathy
> Which, having been, must ever be."

He brooded upon nature, but it was nature mirrored in his own heart. In his poem of "The Brothers" he says of his hero, who had gone to sea:—

> "He had been rear'd
> Among the mountains, and he in his heart
> Was half a shepherd on the stormy seas.
> Oft in the piping shrouds had Leonard heard
> The tones of waterfalls, and inland sounds
> Of caves and trees;"

and, leaning over the vessel's side and gazing into the "broad green wave and sparkling foam," he

> "Saw mountains,—saw the forms of sheep that grazed
> On verdant hills."

This was what his own heart told him; every experience or sentiment called those beloved images to his own mind.

One afternoon, when the sun seemed likely to get the better of the soft rain-clouds, I set out to climb to the top of Helvellyn. I followed the highway a mile or more beyond the Swan Inn, and then I committed myself to a footpath that turns up the mountain-side to the right, and crosses into Grisedale and so to Ulleswater.

Two schoolgirls whom I overtook put me on the right track. The voice of a foaming mountain torrent was in my ears a long distance, and now and then the path crossed it. Fairfield Mountain was on my right hand, Helm Crag and Dunmail Raise on my left. Grasmere plain soon lay far below. The haymakers, encouraged by a gleam of sunshine, were hastily raking together the rain-blackened hay. From my outlook they appeared to be slowly and laboriously rolling up a great sheet of dark brown paper, uncovering beneath it one of the most fresh and vivid green. The mown grass is so long in curing in this country (frequently two weeks) that the new blades spring beneath it, and a second crop is well under way before the old is "carried." The long mountain slopes up which I was making my way were as verdant as the plain below me. Large coarse ferns or bracken, with an under-lining of fine grass, covered the ground on the lower portions. On the higher, grass alone prevailed. On the top of the divide, looking down into the valley of Ulleswater, I came upon one of those black tarns, or mountain lakelets, which are such a feature in this strange scenery. The word "tarn" has no meaning with us, though our young poets sometimes use it as they do this Yorkshire word "wold;" one they get from Wordsworth, the other from Tennyson. But when you have seen one of those still, inky pools at the head of a silent, lonely Westmoreland dale, you will not be apt to misapply the word in future. Suddenly the serene shepherd mountain opens this black, gleaming eye at your feet, and it is all the more weird for having no eyebrow of rocks, or fringe of rush or bush. The steep, encircling slopes drop down and hem it about with the most green and uniform turf. If its rim had been modeled by human hands, it could not have been more regular or gentle in outline. Beneath its emerald coat the soil is black and peaty, which accounts for the hue of the water and the dark line that encircles it.

"All round this pool both flocks and herds might drink
On its firm margin, even as from a well,
Or some stone basin, which the herdsman's hand
Had shaped for their refreshment."

The path led across the outlet of the tarn, and then divided, one branch going down into the head of Grisedale, and the other mounting up the steep flank of Helvellyn. Far up the green acclivity I met a man and two young women making their way slowly down. They had come from Glenridding on Ulleswater, and were going to Grasmere. The women looked cold, and said I would find it wintry on the summit.

Helvellyn has a broad flank and a long back, and comes to a head very slowly and gently. You reach a wire fence well up on the top that divides some sheep ranges, pass through a gate, and have a mile yet to the highest ground in front of you; but you could traverse it in a buggy, it is so smooth and grassy. The grass fails just before the summit is reached, and the ground is covered with small fragments of the decomposed rock. The view is impressive, and such as one likes to sit down to and drink in slowly,—a

"Grand terraqueous spectacle,
From centre to circumference, unveil'd."

The wind was moderate and not cold. Toward Ulleswater the mountain drops down abruptly many hundred feet, but its vast western slope appeared one smooth, unbroken surface of grass. The following jottings in my notebook, on the spot, preserve some of the features of the scene: "All the northern landscape lies in the sunlight as far as Carlisle,

"A tumultuous waste of huge hilltops;"

not quite so severe and rugged as the Scotch mountains, but the view more pleasing and more extensive than the one I got from Ben Venue. The black tarns at my feet,—Keppel Cove Tarn one of them, according to my map,—how curious they look! I can just discern the figure of a man moving by the marge of one of them. Away beyond Ulleswater is a vast sweep of country flecked here and there by slowly moving cloud shadows. To the northeast, in places, the backs and sides of the mountains have a green, pastoral voluptuousness, so smooth and full are they with thick turf. At other points the rock has fretted through the verdant carpet. St. Sunday's Crag to the west, across Grisedale, is a steep acclivity covered with small, loose stones, as if they had been dumped over the top, and were slowly sliding down; but nowhere do I see great bowlders strewn about. Patches of black peat are here and there. The little rills, near and far, are white as milk, so swiftly do they run. On the more precipitous sides the grass and moss are lodged, and hold like snow, and are as tender in hue as the first April blades. A multitude of lakes are in view, and Morecambe Bay to the south. There are sheep everywhere, loosely scattered, with their lambs; occasionally I hear them bleat. No other sound is heard but the chirp of the mountain pipit. I see the wheat-ear flitting here and there. One mountain now lies in full sunshine, as fat as a seal, wrinkled and dimpled where it turns to the west, like a fat animal when it bends to lick itself. What a spectacle is now before me!—all the near mountains in shadow, and the distant in strong sunlight; I shall not see the like of that again. On some of the mountains the green vestments are in tatters and rags, so to speak, and barely cling to them.

No heather in view. Toward Windermere the high peaks and crests are much more jagged and rocky. The air is filled with the same white, motionless vapor as in Scotland. When the sun breaks through,—

"Slant watery lights, from parting clouds, apace
Travel along the precipice's base,
Cheering its naked waste of scatter'd stone."

Amid these scenes one comes face to face with nature,

"With the pristine earth,
The planet in its nakedness,"

as he cannot in a wooded country. The primal, abysmal
energies, grown tender and meditative, as it were, thoughtful
of the shepherd and his flocks, and voiceful only in the leaping
torrents, look out upon one near at hand and pass a mute
recognition. Wordsworth perpetually refers to these hills
and dales as lonely or lonesome; but his heart was still more
lonely. The outward solitude was congenial to the isolation and
profound privacy of his own soul. "Lonesome," he says of one of
these mountain dales, but

"Not melancholy,—no, for it is green
And bright and fertile, furnished in itself
With the few needful things that life requires.
In rugged arms how soft it seems to lie,
How tenderly protected."

It is this tender and sheltering character of the mountains
of the Lake district that is one main source of their charm. So
rugged and lofty, and yet so mellow and delicate! No shaggy,
weedy growths or tangles anywhere; nothing wilder than the
bracken, which at a distance looks as solid as the grass. The turf is
as fine and thick as that of a lawn. The dainty-nosed lambs could
not crave a tenderer bite than it affords. The wool of the dams
could hardly be softer to the foot. The last of July the grass was
still short and thick, as if it never shot up a stalk and produced
seed, but always remained a fine, close mat. Nothing was more

unlike what I was used to at home than this universal tendency (the same is true in Scotland and in Wales) to grass, and, on the lower slopes, to bracken, as if these were the only two plants in nature. Many of these eminences in the north of England, too lofty for hills and too smooth for mountains, are called fells. The railway between Carlisle and Preston winds between them, as Houghill Fells, Tebay Fells, Shap Fells, etc. They are, even in midsummer, of such a vivid and uniform green that it seems as if they must have been painted. Nothing blurs or mars the hue; no stalk of weed or stem of dry grass. The scene, in singleness and purity of tint, rivals the blue of the sky. Nature does not seem to ripen and grow sere as autumn approaches, but wears the tints of May in October.

A Chapter from
Fresh Fields, 1884

WILLIAM WORDSWORTH.

By Henry Cabot Lodge & Francis W. Halsey

Born in 1770; died in 1850; graduated from Cambridge in 1791; traveled on the Continent in 1790-92; settled at Grasmere in 1799; married Mary Hutchinson in 1802; settled at Rydal Mount in 1813; traveled in Scotland in 1814 and in 1832; traveled on the Continent again in 1820 and in 1837; became poet laureate in 1843; published his first volume in 1793 and his last, "The Prelude, in 1850.

A POET DEFINED

Taking up the subject upon general grounds, I ask what is meant by the word Poet? What is a poet? To whom does he address himself? And what language is to be expected from him? He is a man speaking to men: a man, it is true, endued with more lively sensibility, more enthusiasm and tenderness, who has a greater knowledge of human nature, and a more comprehensive soul, than are supposed to be common among mankind; a man pleased with his own passions and volitions, and who rejoices more than other men in the spirit of life that is in him; delighting to contemplate similar volitions and passions as manifested in the goings on of the universe, and habitually impelled to create them where he does not find them. To these qualities he has added a disposition to be affected more than other men by absent things as if they were present; an ability of conjuring up in himself passions, which are indeed far from being the same as those produced by real events, yet especially in those parts of the general sympathy which are pleasing and delightful do more nearly resemble the passions produced by real events than anything which, from the motions of their own minds merely, other men are accustomed to feel in themselves; whence, and from practise, he has acquired a greater readiness and power in expressing what he thinks and feels, and especially those thoughts and feelings which, by his own choice, or from the structure of his own mind, arise in him without immediate external excitement.

But whatever portion of this faculty we may suppose even the greatest poet to possess, there can not be a doubt but that the language which it will suggest to him must, in liveliness and truth, fall far short of that which is uttered by men in real life, under the actual pressure of those passions, certain shadows of which the poet thus produces, or feels to be produced, in himself.

However exalted a notion we would wish to cherish of the character of the poet, it is obvious that, while he describes and imitates passions, his situation is altogether slavish and mechanical, compared with the freedom and power of real and substantial action and suffering. So that it will be the wish of the poet to bring his feelings near to those of the persons whose feelings he describes, nay, for short spaces of time, perhaps, to let himself slip into an entire delusion, and even confound and identify his own feelings with theirs; modifying only the language which is thus suggested to him by a consideration that he describes for a particular purpose, that of giving pleasure. Here, then, he will apply the principle on which I have so much insisted, namely, that of selection; on this he will depend for removing what would otherwise be painful or disgusting in the passion; he will feel that there is no necessity to trick out or elevate nature; and, the more industriously he applies this principle, the deeper will be his faith that no words which his fancy or imagination can suggest will bear to be compared with those which are the emanations of reality and truth.

But it may be said by those who do not object to the general spirit of these remarks, that, as it is impossible for the poet to produce upon all occasions language as exquisitely fitted for the passion as that which the real passion itself suggests, it is proper that he should consider himself as in the situation of a translator, who deems himself justified when he substitutes excellences of another kind for those which are unattainable by him; and endeavors occasionally to surpass his original, in order to make some amends for the general inferiority to which he feels that he must submit. But this would be to encourage idleness and unmanly despair. Further, it is the language of men who speak of what they do not understand; who talk of poetry as of a matter of amusement and idle pleasure; who will converse with us as gravely about a taste for poetry, as they express it, as if it were a thing as indifferent as a taste for rope-dancing, or Frontignac, or Sherry. Aristotle, I have been told, hath said that poetry is the most philosophic of all writing; it is so: its object is truth, not individual and local, but general and operative; not standing upon external testimony, but carried alive into the heart by passion; truth which is its own testimony, which gives strength and divinity to the tribunal to which it appeals, and receives them from the same tribunal. Poetry is the image of man and nature. The obstacles which stand in the way of the fidelity of the biographer and historian, and of their consequent utility, are incalculably greater than those which are to be encountered by the poet who has an adequate notion of the dignity of his art. The poet writes under one restriction only, namely, that of the necessity of giving immediate pleasure to a human being possest of that information which may be expected from him, not as a lawyer, a physician, a mariner, an astronomer, or a natural philosopher, but as a man. Except this one restriction, there is no object standing between the poet and the image of things: between this and the biographer and the historian there are a thousand.

Nor let this necessity of producing immediate pleasure be

considered as a degradation of the poet's art. It is far otherwise. It is an acknowledgment of the beauty of the universe, an acknowledgment the more sincere because it is not formal, but indirect; it is a task light and easy to him who looks at the world in the spirit of love: further, it is an homage paid to the native and naked dignity of man, to the grand elementary principle of pleasure, by which he knows, and feels, and lives, and moves. We have no sympathy but what is propagated by pleasure. I would not be misunderstood, but wherever we sympathize with pain it will be found that the sympathy is produced and carried on by subtle combinations with pleasure. We have no knowledge, that is, no general principles drawn from the contemplation of particular facts, but what has been built up by pleasure, and exists in us by pleasure alone. The man of science, the chemist, and mathematician, whatever difficulties and disgusts they may have had to struggle with, know and feel this. However painful may be the objects with which the anatomist's knowledge is connected, he feels that his knowledge is pleasure; and where he has no pleasure he has no knowledge. What then does the poet? He considers man and the objects that surround him as acting and reacting upon each other, so as to produce an infinite complexity of pain and pleasure; he considers man in his own nature and in his ordinary life as contemplating this with a certain quantity of immediate knowledge, with certain convictions, intuitions, and deductions, which by habit become of the nature of intuitions; he considers him as looking upon this complex scene of ideas and sensations, and finding everywhere objects that immediately excite in him sympathies which, from the necessities of his nature, are accompanied by an overbalance of enjoyment.

To this knowledge which all men carry about with them, and to these sympathies in which, without any other discipline than that of our daily life, we are fitted to take delight, the poet principally directs his attention. He considers man and nature as essentially adapted to each other, and the mind of man as naturally the mirror of the fairest and most interesting qualities of nature. And thus the poet, prompted by this feeling of pleasure which accompanies him through the whole course of his studies, converses with general nature with affections akin to those which, through labor and length of time, the man of science has raised up in himself, by conversing with those parts of nature which are the objects of his studies. The knowledge both of the poet and the man of science is pleasure; but the knowledge of the one cleaves to us as a necessary part of our existence, our natural and unalienable inheritance; the other is a personal and individual acquisition, slow to come to us, and by no habitual and direct sympathy connecting us with our fellow beings. The man of science seeks truth as a remote and unknown benefactor; he cherishes and loves it in his solitude; the poet, singing a song in which all human beings join with him, rejoices in the presence of truth as our visible friend and hourly companion. Poetry is the breath and finer spirit of all knowledge; it is the impassioned expression which is in the countenance of all science. Emphatically may be said of the poet, as Shakespeare hath said of man, "that he looks before and after." He is the rock of defense of human nature, an upholder and preserver, carrying everywhere with him relationship and love. In spite of difference of soil and climate, of language and manners, of laws and customs, in spite of things silently gone out of mind, and things violently destroyed, the poet binds together by passion and knowledge the vast empire of human society, as it is spread over the whole earth and over all time. The objects of the poet's thoughts are everywhere; tho the eyes and senses of man are, it is true, his favorite guides, yet he will follow wheresoever he can find an atmosphere of sensation in which to move his wings. Poetry is the first and last of all knowledge—it is as immortal as the heart of man.

If the labors of men of science should ever create any material revolution, direct or indirect, in our condition, and in the impressions which we habitually receive, the poet will sleep then no more than at present, but he will be ready to follow the steps of the man of science, not only in those general indirect effects, but he will be at his side, carrying sensation into the midst of the science itself. The remotest discoveries of the chemist, the botanist, or mineralogist will be as proper objects of the poet's art as any upon which it can be employed, if the time should ever come when these things shall be familiar to us, and the relations under which they are contemplated by the followers of these respective sciences shall be manifestly and palpably material to us as enjoying and suffering beings. If the time should ever come when what is now called science, thus familiarized to men, shall be ready to put on, as it were, a form of flesh and blood, the poet will lend his divine spirit to aid the transfiguration, and will welcome the being thus produced as a dear and genuine inmate of the household of man. It is not, then, to be supposed that any one, who holds that sublime notion of poetry which I have attempted to convey, will break in upon the sanctity and truth of his pictures by transitory and accidental ornaments, and endeavor to excite admiration of himself by arts, the necessity of which must manifestly depend upon the assumed meanness of his subject.

A CHAPTER FROM
The Best of the World's Classics, Vol. V (of X)
— *Great Britain and Ireland III,* 1909

WORDSWORTH.

By Walter Horatio Pater

SOME English critics at the beginning of the present century had a great deal to say concerning a distinction, of much importance, as they thought, in the true estimate of poetry, between the Fancy, and another more powerful faculty—the Imagination. This metaphysical distinction, borrowed originally from the writings of German philosophers, and perhaps not always clearly apprehended by those who talked of it, involved a far deeper and more vital distinction, with which indeed all true criticism more or less directly has to do, the distinction, namely, between higher and lower degrees of intensity in the poet's perception of his subject, and in his concentration of himself upon his work. Of those who dwelt upon the metaphysical distinction between the Fancy and the Imagination, it was Wordsworth who made the most of it, assuming it as the basis for the final classification of his poetical writings; and it is in these writings that the deeper and more vital distinction, which, as I have said, underlies the metaphysical distinction, is most needed, and may best be illustrated.

For nowhere is there so perplexed a mixture as in Wordsworth's own poetry, of work touched with intense and individual power, with work of almost no character at all. He has much conventional sentiment, and some of that insincere poetic diction, against which his most serious critical efforts were directed: the reaction in his political ideas, consequent on the excesses of 1795, makes him, at times, a mere declaimer on moral and social topics; and he seems, sometimes, to force an

65

unwilling pen, and write by rule. By making the most of these blemishes it is possible to obscure the true aesthetic value of his work, just as his life also, a life of much quiet delicacy and independence, might easily be placed in a false focus, and made to appear a somewhat tame theme in illustration of the more obvious parochial virtues. And those who wish to understand his influence, and experience his peculiar savour, must bear with patience the presence of an alien element in Wordsworth's work, which never coalesced with what is really delightful in it, nor underwent his special power. Who that values his writings most has not felt the intrusion there, from time to time, of something tedious and prosaic? Of all poets equally great, he would gain most by a skilfully made anthology. Such a selection would show, in truth, not so much what he was, or to himself or others seemed to be, as what, by the more energetic and fertile quality in his writings, he was ever tending to become. And the mixture in his work, as it actually stands, is so perplexed, that one fears to miss the least promising composition even, lest some precious morsel should be lying hidden within—the few perfect lines, the phrase, the single word perhaps, to which he often works up mechanically through a poem, almost the whole of which may be tame enough. He who thought that in all creative work the larger part was given passively, to the recipient mind, who waited so dutifully upon the gift, to whom so large a measure was sometimes given, had his times also of desertion and relapse; and he has permitted the impress of these too to remain in his work. And this duality there—the fitfulness with which the higher qualities manifest themselves in it, gives the effect in his poetry of a power not altogether his own, or under his control, which comes and goes when it will, lifting or lowering a matter, poor in itself; so that that old fancy which made the poet's art an enthusiasm, a form of divine possession, seems almost literally true of him.

This constant suggestion of an absolute duality between higher and lower moods, and the work done in them, stimulating one always to look below the surface, makes the reading of Wordsworth an excellent sort of training towards the things of art and poetry. It begets in those, who, coming across him in youth, can bear him at all, a habit of reading between the lines, a faith in the effect of concentration and collectedness of mind in the right appreciation of poetry, an expectation of things, in this order, coming to one by means of a right discipline of the temper as well as of the intellect. He meets us with the promise that he has much, and something very peculiar, to give us, if we will follow a certain difficult way, and seems to have the secret of a special and privileged state of mind. And those who have undergone his influence, and followed this difficult way, are like people who have passed through some initiation, a disciplina arcani, by submitting to which they become able constantly to distinguish in art, speech, feeling, manners, that which is organic, animated, expressive, from that which is only conventional, derivative, inexpressive.

But although the necessity of selecting these precious morsels for oneself is an opportunity for the exercise of Wordsworth's peculiar influence, and induces a kind of just criticism and true estimate of it, yet the purely literary product would have been more excellent, had the writer himself purged away that alien element. How perfect would have been the little treasury, shut between the covers of how thin a book! Let us suppose the desired separation made, the electric thread untwined, the golden pieces, great and small, lying apart together.[1] What are the peculiarities of this residue? What special sense does Wordsworth exercise, and what instincts does he satisfy? What are the subjects and the motives which in him excite the imaginative faculty? What are the qualities in things and persons which he values, the impression and sense of which he can convey to others, in an extraordinary way?

An intimate consciousness of the expression of natural things, which weighs, listens, penetrates, where the earlier mind passed roughly by, is a large element in the complexion of modern poetry. It has been remarked as a fact in mental history again and again. It reveals itself in many forms; but is strongest and most attractive in what is strongest and most attractive in modern literature. It is exemplified, almost equally, by writers as unlike each other as Senancour and Théophile Gautier: as a singular chapter in the history of the human mind, its growth might be traced from Rousseau to Chateaubriand, from Chateaubriand to Victor Hugo: it has doubtless some latent connexion with those pantheistic theories which locate an intelligent soul in material things, and have largely exercised men's minds in some modern systems of philosophy: it is traceable even inthe graver writings of historians: it makes as much difference between ancient and modern landscape art, as there is between the rough masks of an early mosaic and a portrait by Reynolds or Gainsborough. Of this new sense, the writings of Wordsworth are the central and elementary expression: he is more simply and entirely occupied with it than any other poet, though there are fine expressions of precisely the same thing in so different a poet as Shelley. There was in his own character a certain contentment, a sort of inborn religious placidity, seldom found united with a sensibility so mobile as his, which was favourable to the quiet, habitual observation of inanimate, or imperfectly animate, existence. His life of eighty years is divided by no very profoundly felt incidents: its changes are almost wholly inward, and it falls into broad, untroubled, perhaps somewhat monotonous spaces. What it most resembles is the life of one of those early Italian or Flemish painters, who, just because their minds were full of heavenly visions, passed, some of them, the better part of sixty years in quiet, systematic industry. This placid life matured a quite unusual sensibility, really innate in him, to the sights and sounds of the natural world—the flower and its shadow on the stone, the cuckoo and its echo. The poem of Resolution and Independence is a storehouse of such records: for its fulness of imagery it may be compared to Keats's Saint Agnes' Eve. To read one of his longer pastoral poems for the first time, is like a day spent in a new country: the memory is crowded for a while with its precise and vivid incidents—

> The pliant harebell swinging in the breeze
> On some grey rock;—
>
> The single sheep and the one blasted tree
> And the bleak music from that old stone wall;—
>
> In the meadows and the lower ground
> Was all the sweetness of a common dawn;—
>
> And that green corn all day is rustling in thine ears.

Clear and delicate at once, as he is in the outlining of visible imagery, he is more clear and delicate still, and finely scrupulous, in the noting of sounds; so that he conceives of noble sound as even moulding the human countenance to nobler types, and as something actually "profaned" by colour, by visible form, or image.

He has a power likewise of realising, and conveying to the consciousness of the reader, abstract and elementary impressions—silence, darkness, absolute motionlessness: or, again, the whole complex sentiment of a particular place, the abstract expression of desolation in the long white road, of peacefulness in a particular folding of the hills. In the airy building of the brain, a special day or hour even, comes to have for him a sort of personal identity, a spirit or angel given to it, by which, for its exceptional insight, or the happy light upon it, it has a presence in one's history, and acts there, as a separate power or accomplishment; and he has celebrated in many of his poems the "efficacious spirit," which, as he says, resides in these "particular spots" of time.

It is to such a world, and to a world of congruous meditation thereon, that we see him retiring in his but lately published poem of The Recluse—taking leave, without much count of costs, of the world of business, of action and ambition; as also of all that for the majority of mankind counts as sensuous enjoyment.[2]

And so it came about that this sense of a life in natural objects, which in most poetry is but a rhetorical artifice, is with Wordsworth the assertion of what for him is almost literal fact. To him every natural object seemed to possess more or less of a moral or spiritual life, to be capable of a companionship with man, full of expression, of inexplicable affinities and delicacies of intercourse. An emanation, a particular spirit, belonged, not to the moving leaves or water only, but to the distant peak of the hills arising suddenly, by some change of perspective, above the nearer horizon, to the passing space of light across the plain, to the lichened Druidic stone even, for a certain weird fellowship in it with the moods of men. It was like a "survival," in the peculiar intellectual temperament of a man of letters at the end of the eighteenth century, of that primitive condition, which some philosophers have traced in the general history of human culture, wherein all outward objects alike, including even the works of men's hands, were believed to be endowed with animation, and the world was "full of souls"—that mood in which the old Greek gods were first begotten, and which had many strange aftergrowths.

In the early ages, this belief, delightful as its effects on poetry often are, was but the result of a crude intelligence. But, in Wordsworth, such power of seeing life, such perception of a soul, in inanimate things, came of an exceptional susceptibility to the impressions of eye and ear, and was, in its essence, a kind of sensuousness. At least, it is only in a temperament exceptionally susceptible on the sensuous side, that this sense of the expressiveness of outward things comes to be so large a part of life. That he awakened "a sort of thought in sense," is Shelley's just estimate of this element in Wordsworth's poetry.

And it was through nature, thus ennobled by a semblance of passion and thought, that he approached the spectacle of human life. Human life, indeed, is for him, at first, only an additional, accidental grace on an expressive landscape. When he thought of man, it was of man as in the presence and under the influence of these effective natural objects, and linked to them by many associations. The close connexion of man with natural objects, the habitual association of his thoughts and feelings with a particular spot of earth, has sometimes seemed to degrade those who are subject to its influence, as if it did but reinforce that physical connexion of our nature with the actual lime and clay of the soil, which is always drawing us nearer to our end. But for Wordsworth, these influences tended to the dignity of human nature, because they tended to tranquillise it. By raising nature to the level of human thought he gives it power and expression: he subdues man to the level of nature, and gives him thereby a certain breadth and coolness and solemnity. The leech-gatherer on the moor, the woman "stepping westward," are for him natural objects, almost in the same sense as the aged thorn, or the lichened rock on the heath. In this sense the leader of the "Lake School," in spite of an earnest preoccupation with man, his thoughts, his destiny, is the poet of nature. And of nature, after all, in its modesty. The English lake country has, of course, its grandeurs. But the peculiar function of Wordsworth's genius, as carrying in it a power to open out the soul of apparently little or familiar things, would have found its true test had he become the poet of Surrey, say! and the prophet of its life. The glories of Italy and Switzerland, though he did write a little about them, had too potent a material life of their own to serve greatly his poetic purpose.

Religious sentiment, consecrating the affections and natural regrets of the human heart, above all, that pitiful awe and care for the perishing human clay, of which relic-worship is but the corruption, has always had much to do with localities, with the thoughts which attach themselves to actual scenes and places. Now what is true of it everywhere, is truest of it in those secluded valleys where one generation after another maintains the same abiding-place; and it was on this side, that Wordsworth apprehended religion most strongly. Consisting, as it did so much, in the recognition of local sanctities, in the habit of connecting the stones and trees of a particular spot of earth with the great events of life, till the low walls, the green mounds, the half-obliterated epitaphs seemed full of voices, and a sort of natural oracles, the very religion of these people of the dales appeared but as another link between them and the earth, and was literally a religion of nature. It tranquillised them by bringing them under the placid rule of traditional and narrowly localised observances. "Grave livers," they seemed to him, under this aspect, with stately speech, and something of that natural dignity of manners, which underlies the highest courtesy.

And, seeing man thus as a part of nature, elevated and solemnised in proportion as his daily life and occupations brought him into companionship with permanent natural objects, his very religion forming new links for him with the narrow limits of the valley, the low vaults of his church, the rough stones of his home, made intense for him now with profound sentiment, Wordsworth was able to appreciate passion in the lowly. He chooses to depict people from humble life, because, being nearer to nature than others, they are on the whole more impassioned, certainly more direct in their expression of passion, than other men: it is for this direct expression of passion, that he values their humble words. In much that he said in exaltation of rural life, he was but pleading indirectly for that sincerity, that perfect fidelity to one's own inward presentations, to the precise features of the picture within, without which any profound poetry is impossible. It was not for their tameness, but for this passionate sincerity, that he chose incidents and situations from common life, "related in a selection of language really used by men." He constantly endeavours to bring his language near to the real language of men: to the real language of men, however, not on the dead level of their ordinary intercourse, but in select moments of vivid sensation, when this language is winnowed and ennobled by excitement. There are poets who have chosen rural life as their subject, for the sake of its passionless repose, and times when Wordsworth himself extols the mere calm and dispassionate survey of things as the highest aim of poetical culture. But it was not for such passionless calm that he preferred the scenes of pastoral life; and the meditative poet, sheltering himself, as it might seem, from the agitations of the outward world, is in reality only clearing the scene for the great exhibitions of emotion, and what he values most is the almost elementary expression of elementary feelings.

And so he has much for those who value highly the concentrated presentment of passion, who appraise men and women by their susceptibility to it, and art and poetry as they afford the spectacle of it. Breaking from time to time into the pensive spectacle of their daily toil, their occupations near to nature, come those great elementary feelings, lifting and solemnising their language and giving it a natural music. The great, distinguishing passion came to Michael by the sheepfold, to Ruth by the wayside, adding these humble children of the furrow to the true aristocracy of passionate souls. In this respect, Wordsworth's work resembles most that of George Sand, in those of her novels which depict country life. With a penetrative pathos, which puts him in the same rank with the masters of the sentiment of pity in literature, with Meinhold and Victor Hugo, he collects all the traces of vivid excitement which were to be found in that pastoral world—the girl who rung her father's knell; the unborn infant feeling about its mother's heart; the instinctive touches of children; the sorrows of the wild creatures, even—their home-sickness, their strange yearnings; the tales of passionate regret that hang by a ruined farm-building, a heap of stones, a deserted sheepfold; that gay, false, adventurous, outer world, which breaks in from time to time to bewilder and deflower these quiet homes; not "passionate sorrow" only, for the overthrow of the soul's beauty, but the loss of, or carelessness for personal beauty even, in those whom men have wronged—their pathetic wanness; the sailor "who, in his heart, was half a shepherd on the stormy seas"; the wild woman teaching her child to pray for her betrayer; incidents like the making of the shepherd's staff, or that of the young boy laying the first stone of the sheepfold;—all the pathetic episodes of their humble existence, their longing, their wonder at fortune, their poor pathetic pleasures, like the pleasures of children, won so hardly in the struggle for bare existence; their yearning towards each other, in their darkened houses, or at their early toil. A sort of biblical depth and solemnity hangs over this strange, new, passionate, pastoral world, of which he first raised the image, and the reflection of which some of our best modern fiction has caught from him.

He pondered much over the philosophy of his poetry, and reading deeply in the history of his own mind, seems at times to have passed the borders of a world of strange speculations, inconsistent enough, had he cared to note such inconsistencies, with those traditional beliefs, which were otherwise the object of his devout acceptance. Thinking of the high value he set upon customariness, upon all that is habitual, local, rooted in the ground, in matters of religious sentiment, you might sometimes regard him as one tethered down to a world, refined and peaceful indeed, but with no broad outlook, a world protected, but somewhat narrowed, by the influence of received ideas. But he is at times also something very different from this, and something much bolder. A chance expression is overheard and placed in a new connexion, the sudden memory of a thing long past occurs to him, a distant object is relieved for a while by a random gleam of light—accidents turning up for a moment what lies below the surface of our immediate experience—and he passes from the humble graves and lowly arches of "the little rock-like pile" of a Westmoreland church, on bold trains of speculative thought, and comes, from point to point, into strange contact with thoughts which have visited, from time to time, far more venturesome, perhaps errant, spirits.

He had pondered deeply, for instance, on those strange

reminiscences and forebodings, which seem to make our lives stretch before and behind us, beyond where we can see or touch anything, or trace the lines of connexion. Following the soul, backwards and forwards, on these endless ways, his sense of man's dim, potential powers became a pledge to him, indeed, of a future life, but carried him back also to that mysterious notion of an earlier state of existence—the fancy of the Platonists—the old heresy of Origen. It was in this mood that he conceived those oft-reiterated regrets for a half-ideal childhood, when the relics of Paradise still clung about the soul—a childhood, as it seemed, full of the fruits of old age, lost for all, in a degree, in the passing away of the youth of the world, lost for each one, over again, in the passing away of actual youth. It is this ideal childhood which he celebrates in his famous Ode on the Recollections of Childhood, and some other poems which may be grouped around it, such as the lines on Tintern Abbey, and something like what he describes was actually truer of himself than he seems to have understood; for his own most delightful poems were really the instinctive productions of earlier life, and most surely for him, "the first diviner influence of this world" passed away, more and more completely, in his contact with experience.

Sometimes as he dwelt upon those moments of profound, imaginative power, in which the outward object appears to take colour and expression, a new nature almost, from the prompting of the observant mind, the actual world would, as it were, dissolve and detach itself, flake by flake, and he himself seemed to be the creator, and when he would the destroyer, of the world in which he lived—that old isolating thought of many a brain-sick mystic of ancient and modern times.

At other times, again, in those periods of intense susceptibility, in which he appeared to himself as but the passive recipient of external influences, he was attracted by the thought of a spirit of life in outward things, a single, all-pervading mind in them, of which man, and even the poet's imaginative energy, are but moments—that old dream of the anima mundi, the mother of all things and their grave, in which some had desired to lose themselves, and others had become indifferent to the distinctions of good and evil. It would come, sometimes, like the sign of the macrocosm to Faust in his cell: the network of man and nature was seen to be pervaded by a common, universal life: a new, bold thought lifted him above the furrow, above the green turf of the Westmoreland churchyard, to a world altogether different in its vagueness and vastness, and the narrow glen was full of the brooding power of one universal spirit.

And so he has something, also, for those who feel the fascination of bold speculative ideas, who are really capable of rising upon them to conditions of poetical thought. He uses them, indeed, always with a very fine apprehension of the limits within which alone philosophical imaginings have any place in true poetry; and using them only for poetical purposes, is not too careful even to make them consistent with each other. To him, theories which for other men bring a world of technical diction, brought perfect form and expression, as in those two lofty books of The Prelude, which describe the decay and the restoration of Imagination and Taste. Skirting the borders of this world of bewildering heights and depths, he got but the first exciting influence of it, that joyful enthusiasm which great imaginative theories prompt, when the mind first comes to have an understanding of them; and it is not under the influence of these thoughts that his poetry becomes tedious or loses its blitheness. He keeps them, too, always within certain ethical bounds, so that no word of his could offend the simplest of those simple souls which are always the largest portion of mankind. But it is, nevertheless, the contact of these thoughts, the speculative boldness in them, which constitutes, at least for some minds, the secret attraction of much of his best poetry—the sudden passage from lowly thoughts and places to the majestic forms of philosophical imagination, the play of these forms over a world so different, enlarging so strangely the bounds of its humble churchyards, and breaking such a wild light on the graves of christened children.

And these moods always brought with them faultless expression. In regard to expression, as with feeling and thought, the duality of the higher and lower moods was absolute. It belonged to the higher, the imaginative mood, and was the pledge of its reality, to bring the appropriate language with it. In him, when the really poetical motive worked at all, it united, with absolute justice, the word and the idea; each, in the imaginative flame, becoming inseparably one with the other, by that fusion of matter and form, which is the characteristic of the highest poetical expression. His words are themselves thought and feeling; not eloquent, or musical words merely, but that sort of creative language which carries the reality of what it depicts, directly, to the consciousness.

The music of mere metre performs but a limited, yet a very peculiar and subtly ascertained function, in Wordsworth's poetry. With him, metre is but an additional grace, accessory to that deeper music of words and sounds, that moving power, which they exercise in the nobler prose no less than in formal poetry. It is a sedative to that excitement, an excitement sometimes almost painful, under which the language, alike of poetry and prose, attains a rhythmical power, independent of metrical combination, and dependent rather on some subtle adjustment of the elementary sounds of words themselves to the image or feeling they convey. Yet some of his pieces, pieces prompted by a sort of half-playful mysticism, like the Daffodils and The Two April Mornings, are distinguished by a certain quaint gaiety of metre, and rival by their perfect execution, in this respect, similar pieces among our own Elizabethan, or contemporary French poetry.

And those who take up these poems after an interval of months, or years perhaps, may be surprised at finding how well old favourites wear, how their strange, inventive turns of diction or thought still send through them the old feeling of surprise. Those who lived about Wordsworth were all great lovers of the older English literature, and oftentimes there came out in him a noticeable likeness to our earlier poets. He quotes unconsciously, but with new power of meaning, a clause from one of Shakespeare's sonnets; and, as with some other men's most famous work, the Ode on the Recollections of Childhood had its anticipator.[3] He drew something too from the unconscious mysticism of the old English language itself, drawing out the inward significance of its racy idiom, and the not wholly unconscious poetry of the language used by the simplest people under strong excitement—language, therefore, at its origin.

The office of the poet is not that of the moralist, and the first aim of Wordsworth's poetry is to give the reader a peculiar kind of pleasure. But through his poetry, and through this pleasure in it, he does actually convey to the reader an extraordinary wisdom in the things of practice. One lesson, if men must have lessons, he conveys more clearly than all, the supreme importance of contemplation in the conduct of life.

Contemplation—impassioned contemplation that, is with Wordsworth the end-in-itself, the perfect end. We see the majority of mankind going most often to definite ends, lower or higher ends, as their own instincts may determine; but the end may never be attained, and the means not be quite the right means, great ends and little ones alike being, for the most part, distant, and the ways to them, in this dim world, somewhat vague. Meantime, to higher or lower ends, they move too often with something of a sad countenance, with hurried and ignoble gait, becoming, unconsciously, something like thorns, in their anxiety to bear grapes; it being possible for people, in the pursuit of even great ends, to become themselves thin and impoverished in spirit and temper, thus diminishing the sum of perfection in the world, at its very sources. We understand this when it is a question of mean, or of intensely selfish ends—of Grandet, or Javert. We think it bad morality to say that the end justifies the means, and we know how false to all higher conceptions of the religious life is the type of one who is ready to do evil that good may come. We contrast with such dark, mistaken eagerness, a type like that of Saint Catherine of Siena, who made the means to her ends so attractive, that she has won for herself an undying place in the House Beautiful, not by her rectitude of soul only, but by its "fairness"—by those quite different qualities which commend themselves to the poet and the artist.

Yet, for most of us, the conception of means and ends covers the whole of life, and is the exclusive type or figure under which we represent our lives to ourselves. Such a figure, reducing all things to machinery, though it has on its side the authority of that old Greek moralist who has fixed for succeeding generations the outline of the theory of right living, is too like a mere picture or description of men's lives as we actually find them, to be the basis of the higher ethics. It covers the meanness of men's daily lives, and much of the dexterity with which they pursue what may seem to them the good of themselves or of others; but not the intangible perfection of those whose ideal is rather in being than in doing—not those manners which are, in the deepest as in the simplest sense, morals, and without which one cannot so much as offer a cup of water to a poor man without offence—not the part of "antique Rachel," sitting in the company of Beatrice; and even the moralist might well endeavour rather to withdraw men from the too exclusive consideration of means and ends, in life.

Against this predominance of machinery in our existence, Wordsworth's poetry, like all great art and poetry, is a continual protest. Justify rather the end by the means, it seems to say: whatever may become of the fruit, make sure of the flowers and the leaves. It was justly said, therefore, by one who had meditated very profoundly on the true relation of means to ends in life, and on the distinction between what is desirable in itself and what is desirable only as machinery, that when the battle which he and his friends were waging had been won, the world would need more than ever those qualities which Wordsworth was keeping alive and nourishing.[4]

That the end of life is not action but contemplation—being

as distinct from doing—a certain disposition of the mind: is, in some shape or other, the principle of all the higher morality. In poetry, in art, if you enter into their true spirit at all; you touch this principle, in a measure: these, by their very sterility, are a type of beholding for the mere joy of beholding. To treat life in the spirit of art, is to make life a thing in which means and ends are identified: to encourage such treatment, the true moral significance of art and poetry. Wordsworth, and other poets who have been like him in ancient or more recent times, are the masters, the experts, in this art of impassioned contemplation. Their work is, not to teach lessons, or enforce rules, or even to stimulate us to noble ends; but to withdraw the thoughts for a little while from the mere machinery of life, to fix them, with appropriate emotions, on the spectacle of those great facts in man's existence which no machinery affects, "on the great and universal passions of men, the most general and interesting of their occupations, and the entire world of nature,"—on "the operations of the elements and the appearances of the visible universe, on storm and sunshine, on the revolutions of the seasons, on cold and heat, on loss of friends and kindred, on injuries and resentments, on gratitude and hope, on fear and sorrow." To witness this spectacle with appropriate emotions is the aim of all culture; and of these emotions poetry like Wordsworth's is a great nourisher and stimulant. He sees nature full of sentiment and excitement; he sees men and women as parts of nature, passionate, excited, in strange grouping and connexion with the grandeur and beauty of the natural world:— images, in his own words, "of man suffering, amid awful forms and powers."

Such is the figure of the more powerful and original poet, hidden away, in part, under those weaker elements in Wordsworth's poetry, which for some minds determine their entire character; a poet somewhat bolder and more passionate than might at first sight be supposed, but not too bold for true poetical taste; an unimpassioned writer, you might sometimes fancy, yet thinking the chief aim, in life and art alike, to be a certain deep emotion; seeking most often the great elementary passions in lowly places; having at least this condition of all impassioned work, that he aims always at an absolute sincerity of feeling and diction, so that he is the true forerunner of the deepest and most passionate poetry of our own day; yet going back also, with something of a protest against the conventional fervour of much of the poetry popular in his own time, to those older English poets, whose unconscious likeness often comes out in him.

A CHAPTER FROM
Appreciations,
with an Essay on Style, 1889

FOOTNOTES:

[1] Since this essay was written, such selections have been made, with excellent taste, by Matthew Arnold and Professor Knight.

[2] In Wordsworth's prefatory advertisement to the first edition of The Prelude, published in 1850, it is stated that that work was intended to be introductory to The Recluse; and that The Recluse, if completed, would have consisted of three parts. The second part is The Excursion. The third part was only planned; but the first book of the first part was left in manuscript by Wordsworth—though in manuscript, it is said, in no great condition of forwardness for the printers. This book, now for the first time printed in extenso (a very noble passage from it found place in that prose advertisement to The Excursion), is included in the latest edition of Wordsworth by Mr. John Morley. It was well worth adding to the poet's great bequest to English literature. A true student of his work, who has formulated for himself what he supposes to be the leading

characteristics of Wordsworth's genius, will feel, we think, lively interest in testing them by the various fine passages in what is here presented for the first time. Let the following serve for a sample:—

Thickets full of songsters, and the voice
Of lordly birds, an unexpected sound
Heard now and then from morn to latest eve,
Admonishing the man who walks below
Of solitude and silence in the sky:—
These have we, and a thousand nooks of earth
Have also these, but nowhere else is found,
Nowhere (or is it fancy?) can be found
The one sensation that is here; 'tis here,
Here as it found its way into my heart
In childhood, here as it abides by day,
By night, here only; or in chosen minds
That take it with them hence, where'er they go.
—'Tis, but I cannot name it, 'tis the sense
Of majesty, and beauty, and repose,
A blended holiness of earth and sky,
Something that makes this individual spot,
This small abiding-place of many men,
A termination, and a last retreat,
A centre, come from wheresoe'er you will,
A whole without dependence or defect,
Made for itself, and happy in itself,
Perfect contentment, Unity entire.

[3] Henry Vaughan, in The Retreat.
[4] See an interesting paper, by Mr. John Morley, on "The Death of Mr. Mill," Fortnightly Review, June 1873.

THE ENGLISH LAKES.

By F. W. H. Myers

The lakes and mountains of Cumberland, Westmoreland, and Lancashire, are singularly fitted to supply such elements of moral sustenance as Nature's aspects can afford to man. There are, indeed, many mountain regions of greater awfulness; but prospects of ice and terror should be a rare stimulant rather than an habitual food; and the physical difficulties inseparable from immense elevations depress the inhabitant and preoccupy the traveller. There are many lakes under a more lustrous sky; but the healthy activities of life demand a scene brilliant without languor, and a beauty which can refresh and satisfy rather than lull or overpower. Without advancing any untenable claim to British pre-eminence in the matter of scenery, we may, perhaps, follow on both these points the judgment which Wordsworth has expressed in his *Guide to the Lakes*, a work which condenses the results of many years of intimate observation.

"Our tracts of wood and water," he says, "are almost diminutive in comparison (with Switzerland); therefore, as far as sublimity is dependent upon absolute bulk and height, and atmospherical influences in connexion with these, it is obvious that there can be no rivalship. But a short residence among the British mountains will furnish abundant proof, that, after a certain point of elevation, viz., that which allows of compact and fleecy clouds settling upon, or sweeping over, the summits, the sense of sublimity depends more upon form and relation of objects to each other than upon their actual magnitude; and that an elevation of 3000 feet is sufficient to call forth in a most impressive degree the creative, and magnifying, and softening powers of the atmosphere."

And again, as to climate; "The rain," he says, "here comes down heartily, and is frequently succeeded by clear bright weather, when every brook is vocal, and every torrent sonorous; brooks and torrents which are never muddy even in the heaviest floods. Days of unsettled weather, with partial showers, are very frequent; but the showers, darkening or brightening as they fly from hill to hill, are not less grateful to the eye than finely interwoven passages of gay and sad music are touching to the ear. Vapours exhaling from the lakes and meadows after sunrise in a hot season, or in moist weather brooding upon the heights, or descending towards the valleys with inaudible motion, give a visionary character to everything around them; and are in themselves so beautiful as to dispose us to enter into the feelings of those simple nations (such as the Laplanders of this day) by whom they are taken for guardian deities of the mountains; or to sympathize with others who have fancied these delicate apparitions to be the spirits of their departed ancestors. Akin to these are fleecy clouds resting upon the hill-tops; they are not easily managed in picture, with their accompaniments of blue sky, but how glorious are they in nature! How pregnant with imagination for the poet! And the height of the Cumbrian mountains is sufficient to exhibit daily and hourly instances of those mysterious attachments. Such clouds, cleaving to their stations, or lifting up suddenly their glittering heads from behind rocky barriers, or hurrying out of sight with speed of the sharpest edge, will often tempt an inhabitant to congratulate himself on belonging to a country of mists and clouds and storms, and make him think of the blank sky of Egypt, and of the cerulean vacancy of Italy, as an unanimated and even a sad spectacle."

The consciousness of a preceding turmoil brings home to us best the sense of perfect peace; and a climate accustomed to storm-cloud and tempest can melt sometimes into "a day as still as heaven" with a benignant tranquillity which calmer regions can scarcely know. Such a day Wordsworth has described in language of such delicate truth and beauty as only a long and intimate love can inspire:

"It has been said that in human life there are moments worth ages. In a more subdued tone of sympathy may we affirm, that in the climate of England there are, for the lover of Nature, days which are worth whole months, I might say, even years. One of these favoured days sometimes occurs in springtime, when that soft air is breathing over the blossoms and new-born verdure which inspired Buchanan with his beautiful Ode to the First of May; the air which, in the luxuriance of his fancy, he likens to that of the golden age,— to that which gives motion to the funereal cypresses on the banks of Lethe; to the air which is to salute beatified spirits when expiatory fires shall have consumed the earth with all her habitations. But it is in autumn that days of such affecting influence most frequently intervene. The atmosphere seems refined, and the sky rendered more crystalline, as the vivifying heat of the year abates; the lights and shadows are more delicate; the colouring is richer and more finely harmonized; and, in this season of stillness, the ear being unoccupied, or only gently excited, the sense of vision becomes more susceptible of its appropriate enjoyments. A resident in a country like this which we are treating of will agree with me that the presence of a lake is indispensable to exhibit in perfection the beauty of one of these days; and he must have experienced, while looking on the unruffled waters, that the imagination by their aid is carried into recesses of feeling otherwise impenetrable. The reason of this is, that the heavens are not only brought down into the bosom of the earth, but that the earth is mainly looked at, and thought of, through the medium of a purer element. The happiest time is when the equinoctial gales are departed; but their fury may probably be called to mind by the sight of a few shattered boughs, whose leaves do not differ in colour from the faded foliage of the stately oaks from which these relics of the storm depend: all else speaks of tranquillity; not a breath of air,

no restlessness of insects, and not a moving object perceptible—
except the clouds gliding in the depths of the lake, or the traveller
passing along, an inverted image, whose motion seems governed
by the quiet of a time to which its archetype, the living person,
is perhaps insensible; or it may happen that the figure of one of
the larger birds, a raven or a heron, is crossing silently among the
reflected clouds, while the voice of the real bird, from the element
aloft, gently awakens in the spectator the recollection of appetites
and instincts, pursuits and occupations, that deform and agitate
the world, yet have no power to prevent nature from putting on
an aspect capable of satisfying the most intense cravings for the
tranquil, the lovely, and the perfect, to which man, the noblest of
her creatures, is subject."

The scene described here is one as exquisite in detail as
majestic in general effect. And it is characteristic of the region
to which Wordsworth's love was given that there is no corner
of it without a meaning and a charm; that the open record of
its immemorial past tells us at every turn that all agencies have
conspired for loveliness and ruin itself has been benign. A
passage of Wordsworth's describing the character of the lake-
shores illustrates this fact with loving minuteness.

"Sublimity is the result of nature's first great dealings with
the superficies of the Earth; but the general tendency of her
subsequent operations is towards the production of beauty, by a
multiplicity of symmetrical parts uniting in a consistent whole.
This is everywhere exemplified along the margins of these lakes.
Masses of rock, that have been precipitated from the heights into
the area of waters, lie in some places like stranded ships, or have
acquired the compact structure of jutting piers, or project in
little peninsulas crested with native wood. The smallest rivulet,
one whose silent influx is scarcely noticeable in a season of dry
weather, so faint is the dimple made by it on the surface of the
smooth lake, will be found to have been not useless in shaping,
by its deposits of gravel and soil in time of flood, a curve that
would not otherwise have existed. But the more powerful brooks,

encroaching upon the level of the lake, have, in course of time, given birth to ample promontories of sweeping outline, that contrast boldly with the longitudinal base of the steeps on the opposite shore; while their flat or gently-sloping surfaces never fail to introduce, into the midst of desolation and barrenness, the elements of fertility, even where the habitations of men may not have been raised."

With this we may contrast, as a companion picture, the poet's description of the tarns, or lonely bodies of water, which lie here and there among the hills:

"They are difficult of access and naked; yet some of them are, in their permanent forms, very grand, and there are accidents of things which would make the meanest of them interesting. At all events, one of these pools is an acceptable sight to the mountain wanderer, not merely as an incident that diversifies the prospect, but as forming in his mind a centre or conspicuous point to which objects, otherwise disconnected or insubordinated, may be referred. Some few have a varied outline, with bold heath-clad promontories; and as they mostly lie at the foot of a steep precipice, the water, where the sun is not shining upon it, appears black and sullen, and round the margin huge stones and masses of rock are scattered, some defying conjecture as to the means by which they came thither, and others obviously fallen from on high, the contribution of ages! A not unpleasing sadness is induced by this perplexity, and these images of decay; while the prospect of a body of pure water, unattended with groves and other cheerful rural images by which fresh water is usually accompanied, and unable to give furtherance to the meagre vegetation around it, excites a sense of some repulsive power strongly put forth, and thus deepens the melancholy natural to such scenes."

To those who love to deduce the character of a population from the character of their race and surroundings the peasantry of Cumberland and Westmoreland form an attractive theme. Drawn in great part from the strong Scandinavian stock, they dwell in a land solemn and beautiful as Norway itself, but without Norway's rigour and penury, and with still lakes and happy rivers instead of Norway's inarming melancholy sea. They are a mountain folk; but their mountains are no precipices of insuperable snow, such as keep the dwellers in some Swiss hamlet shut in ignorance and stagnating into idiocy. These barriers divide only to concentrate, and environ only to endear; their guardianship is but enough to give an added unity to each group of kindred homes. And thus it is that the Cumbrian dalesmen have afforded perhaps as near a realization as human fates have yet allowed of the rural society which statesmen desire for their country's greatness. They have given an example of substantial comfort strenuously won; of home affections intensified by independent strength; of isolation without ignorance, and of a shrewd simplicity; of an hereditary virtue which needs no support from fanaticism, and to which honour is more than law.

The school of political economists, moreover, who urge the advantage of a peasant proprietary—of small independent holdings,—as at once drawing from the land the fullest produce and rearing upon it the most vigorous and provident population,—this school, as is well known, finds in the *statesmen* of Cumberland one of its favourite examples. In the days of border-wars, when the first object was to secure the existence of as many armed men as possible, in readiness to repel the Scot, the abbeys and great proprietors in the north readily granted small estates on military tenure, which tenure, when personal service in the field was no longer needed, became in most cases an absolute ownership. The attachment of these *statesmen* to their hereditary estates, the heroic efforts which they would make to avoid parting with them, formed an impressive phenomenon in the little world—a world at once of equality and of conservatism—which was the scene of Wordsworth's childish years, and which remained his manhood's ideal.

The growth of large fortunes in England, and the increased competition for land, has swallowed up many of these small independent holdings in the extensive properties of wealthy men.

And at the same time the spread of education, and the improved poor-laws and other legislation, by raising the condition of other parts of England, have tended to obliterate the contrast which was so marked in Wordsworth's day. How marked that contrast was, a comparison of Crabbe's poems with Wordsworth's will sufficiently indicate. Both are true painters; but while in the one we see poverty as something gross and degrading, and the *Tales of the Village* stand out from a background of pauperism and crime; in the other picture poverty means nothing worse than privation, and the poet in the presence of the most tragic outcast of fortune could still

> Have laughed himself to scorn, to find
> In that decrepit man so firm a mind.

Nay, even when a state far below the *Leech-Gatherer's* has been reached, and mind and body alike are in their last decay, the life of the *Old Cumberland Beggar*, at one remove from nothingness, has yet a dignity and a usefulness of its own. His fading days are passed in no sad asylum of vicious or gloomy age, but amid neighbourly kindnesses, and in the sanity of the open air; and a life that is reduced to its barest elements has yet a hold on the liberality of nature and the affections of human hearts.

So long as the inhabitants of a region thus solitary and beautiful have neither many arts nor many wishes, save such as the Nature which they know has suggested, and their own handiwork can satisfy, so long are their presence and habitations likely to be in harmony with the scenes around them. Nay, man's presence is almost always needed to draw out the full meaning of Nature, to illustrate her bounty by his glad well-being and to hint by his contrivances of precaution at her might and terror. Wordsworth's description of the cottages of Cumberland depicts this unconscious adaptation of man's abode to his surroundings, with an eye which may be called at pleasure that of painter or of poet.

"The dwelling-houses, and contiguous outhouses, are in many instances of the colour of the native rock out of which they have been built; but frequently the dwelling—or Fire-house, as it is ordinarily called—has been distinguished from the barn or byre by roughcast and whitewash, which, as the inhabitants are not hasty in renewing it, in a few years acquires by the influence of weather a tint at once sober and variegated. As these houses have been, from father to son, inhabited by persons engaged in the same occupations, yet necessarily with changes in their circumstances, they have received without incongruity additions and accommodations adapted to the needs of each successive occupant, who, being for the most part proprietor, was at liberty to follow his own fancy, so that these humble dwellings remind the contemplative spectator of a production of Nature, and may (using a strong expression) rather be said to have grown than to have been erected—to have risen, by an instinct of their own, out of the native rock—so little is there in them of formality, such is their wildness and beauty."

"These dwellings, mostly built, as has been said, of rough unhewn stone, are roofed with slates, which were rudely taken from the quarry before the present art of splitting them was understood, and are therefore rough and uneven in their surface, so that both the coverings and sides of the houses have furnished places of rest for the seeds of lichens, mosses, ferns and flowers. Hence buildings, which in their very form call to mind the processes of Nature, do thus, clothed in part with a vegetable garb, appear to be received into the bosom of the living principle of things, as it acts and exists among the woods and fields, and by their colour and their shape affectingly direct the thoughts to that tranquil course of nature and simplicity along which the humble-minded inhabitants have through so many generations been led. Add the little garden with its shed for bee-hives, its small bed of potherbs, and its borders and patches of flowers for Sunday posies, with sometimes a choice few too much prized to be plucked; an orchard of proportioned size; a cheesepress, often supported by some tree near the door; a cluster of embowering sycamores for summer shade, with a tall fir through which the winds sing when other trees are leafless; the little rill or household spout murmuring in all seasons,—combine these incidents and images together, and you have the representative idea of a mountain cottage in this country—so beautifully formed in itself, and so richly adorned by the hand of Nature."

These brief descriptions may suffice to indicate the general character of a district which in Wordsworth's early days had a distinctive unity which he was the first fully to appreciate, which was at its best during his long lifetime, and which has already begun to disappear. The mountains had waited long for a full adoration, an intelligent worship. At last "they were enough beloved." And if now the changes wrought around them recall too often the poet's warning, how

> All that now delights thee, from the day
> On which it should be touched, shall
> melt, and melt away,—

yet they have gained something which cannot be taken from them. Not mines, nor railways, nor monster excursions, nor reservoirs, nor Manchester herself, "toute entière à sa proie attachée," can deprive lake and hill of Wordsworth's memory, and the love which once they knew.

Wordsworth's life was from the very first so ordered as to give him the most complete and intimate knowledge both of district and people. There was scarcely a mile of ground in the Lake country over which he had not wandered; scarcely a prospect which was not linked with his life by some tie of memory. Born at Cockermouth, on the outskirts of the district, his mind was gradually led on to its beauty; and his first recollections were of Derwent's grassy holms and rocky falls, with Skiddaw, "bronzed with deepest radiance," towering in the eastern sky. Sent to school at Hawkshead at eight years old, Wordsworth's scene

91

was transferred to the other extremity of the lake district. It was in this quaint old town, on the banks of Esthwaite Water, that the "fair seed-time of his soul" was passed; it was here that his boyish delight in exercise and adventure grew, and melted in its turn into a more impersonal yearning, a deeper absorption into the beauty and the wonder of the world. And even the records of his boyish amusements come to us each on a background of Nature's majesty and calm. Setting springs for woodcock on the grassy moors at night, at nine years old, he feels himself "a trouble to the peace" that dwells among the moon and stars overhead; and when he has appropriated a woodcock caught by somebody else, "sounds of undistinguishable motion" embody the viewless pursuit of Nemesis among the solitary hills. In the perilous search for the raven's nest, as he hangs on the face of the naked crags of Yewdale, he feels for the first time that sense of detachment from external things which a position of strange unreality will often force on the mind.

> Oh, at that time
> When on the perilous ridge I hung alone,
> With what strange utterance did the loud dry wind
> Blow through my ear! The sky seemed not a sky
> Of earth—and with what motion moved the clouds!

The innocent rapine of *nutting* taught him to feel that there is a spirit in the woods—a presence which too rude a touch of ours will desecrate and destroy.

The neighbouring lakes of Coniston, Esthwaite, Windermere, have left similar traces of the gradual upbuilding of his spirit. It was on a promontory on Coniston that the sun's last rays, gilding the eastern hills above which he had first appeared, suggested the boy's first impulse of spontaneous poetry, in the resolve that, wherever life should lead him, his last thoughts should fall on the scenes where his childhood was passing now. It was on Esthwaite that the "huge peak" of Wetherlam, following him (as it seemed) as he rowed across the starlit water, suggested the dim conception of "unknown modes of being," and a life that is not ours. It was round Esthwaite that the boy used to wander with a friend at early dawn, rejoicing in the charm of words in tuneful order, and repeating together their favourite verses, till "sounds of exultation echoed through the groves." It was on Esthwaite that the band of skaters "hissed along the polished ice in games confederate," from which Wordsworth would sometimes withdraw himself and pause suddenly in full career, to feel in that dizzy silence the mystery of a rolling world.

A passage, less frequently quoted, in describing a boating excursion on Windermere illustrates the effect of some small point of human interest in concentrating and realising the diffused emotion which radiates from a scene of beauty:

> But, ere nightfall,
> When in our pinnace we returned at leisure
> Over the shadowy lake, and to the beach
> Of some small island steered our course with one,
> The minstrel of the troop, and left him there,
> And rowed off gently, while he blew his flute
> Alone upon the rock—oh, then the calm
> And dead still water lay upon my mind
> Even with a weight of pleasure, and the sky,
> Never before so beautiful, sank down
> Into my heart, and held me like a dream!

The passage which describes the schoolboy's call to the owls— the lines of which Coleridge said that he should have exclaimed "Wordsworth!" if he had met them running wild in the deserts of Arabia,—paint a somewhat similar rush of feeling with a still deeper charm. The "gentle shock of mild surprise" which in the pauses of the birds' jocund din *carries far into his heart the sound of mountain torrents*—the very mingling of the grotesque and the majestic—brings home the contrast between our transitory energies and the mystery around us which returns ever the same to the moments when we pause and are at peace.

It is round the two small lakes of Grasmere and Rydal that the memories of Wordsworth are most thickly clustered. On one or other of these lakes he lived for fifty years,—the first half of the present century; and there is not in all that region a hillside walk or winding valley which has not heard him murmuring out his verses as they slowly rose from his heart. The cottage at Townend, Grasmere, where he first settled, is now surrounded by the out-buildings of a busy hotel; and the noisy stream of traffic, and the sight of the many villas which spot the valley, give a new pathos to the sonnet in which Wordsworth deplores the alteration which even his own residence might make in the simplicity of the lonely scene.

> Well may'st thou halt, and gaze with brightening eye!
> The lovely Cottage in the guardian nook
> Hath stirred thee deeply; with its own dear brook,
> Its own small pasture, almost its own sky!
> But covet not the Abode: forbear to sigh,
> As many do, repining while they look;
> Intruders—who would tear from Nature's book
> This precious leaf with harsh impiety.
> Think what the home must be if it were thine,
> Even thine, though few thy wants! Roof, window, door,
> The very flowers are sacred to the Poor,
> The roses to the porch which they entwine:
> Yea, all that now enchants thee, from the day
> On which it should be touched, would
>   melt, and melt away.

The *Poems on the Naming of Places* belong for the most part to this neighbourhood. *Emma's Dell* on Easdale Beck, *Point Rash-Judgment* on the eastern shore of Grasmere, *Mary's Pool* in Rydal Park, *William's Peak* on Stone Arthur, *Joanna's Rock* on the banks of Rotha, and *John's Grove* near White Moss Common, have been identified by the loving search of those to whom every memorial of that simple-hearted family group has still a charm.

It is on Greenhead Ghyll—"upon the forest-side in Grasmere Vale"— that the poet has laid the scene of *Michael,* the poem which paints with such detailed fidelity both the inner and the outward life of a typical Westmoreland "statesman." And the upper road from Grasmere to Rydal, superseded now by the road along the lake side, and left as a winding footpath among rock and fern, was one of his most habitual haunts. Of another such haunt his friend Lady Richardson says, "The *Prelude* was chiefly composed in a green mountain terrace, on the Easdale side of Helm Crag, known by the name of Under Lancrigg, a place which he used to say he knew by heart. The ladies sat at their work on the hill-side, while he walked to and fro on the smooth green mountain turf, humming out his verses to himself, and then repeating them to his sympathising and ready scribes, to be noted down on the spot, and transcribed at home."

The neighbourhood of the poet's later home at Rydal Mount is equally full of associations. Two of the *Evening Voluntaries* were composed by the side of Rydal Mere. The *Wild Duck's Nest* was on one of the Rydal islands. It was on the fells of Loughrigg that the poet's fancy loved to plant an imperial castle. And *Wansfell's* green slope still answers with many a change of glow and shadow to the radiance of the sinking sun.

Hawkshead and Rydal, then, may be considered as the poet's principal centres, and the scenery in their neighbourhood has received his most frequent attention. The Duddon, a seldom-visited stream on the south-west border of the Lake-district, has been traced by him from source to outfall in a series of sonnets. Langdale, and Little Langdale with Blea Tarn lying in it, form the principal scene of the discourses in the *Excursion.* The more distant lakes and mountains were often visited and are often alluded to. The scene of *The Brothers,* for example, is laid in Ennerdale; and the index of the minor poems will supply other instances. But it is chiefly round two lines of road leading from Grasmere that Wordsworth's associations cluster,—the route over Dunmailraise, which led him to Keswick, to Coleridge and Southey at Greta Hall, and to other friends in that neighbourhood; and the route over Kirkstone, which led him to Ullswater, and the friendly houses of Patterdale, Hallsteads, and Lowther Castle. The first of these two routes was that over which the *Waggoner* plied; it skirts the lovely shore of Thirlmere,—a lonely sheet of water, of exquisite irregularity of outline, and fringed with delicate verdure, which the Corporation of Manchester has lately bought to embank it into a reservoir.

Dedecorum pretiosus emptor! This lake was a favourite haunt of Wordsworth's; and upon a rock on its margin, where he and Coleridge, coming from Keswick and Grasmere, would often meet, the two poets, with the other members of Wordsworth's loving household group, inscribed the initial letters of their names. To the "monumental power" of this Rock of Names Wordsworth appeals, in lines written when the happy company who engraved them had already been severed by distance and death;

> O thought of pain,
> That would impair it or profane!
> And fail not Thou, loved Rock, to keep
> Thy charge when we are laid asleep.

The rock may still be seen, but is to be submerged in the new reservoir. In the vale of Keswick itself, Applethwaite, Skiddaw, St. Herbert's Island, Lodore, are commemorated in sonnets or inscriptions. And the Borrowdale yew-trees have inspired some of the poet's noblest lines,—lines breathing all the strange forlornness of Glaramara's solitude, and the withering vault of shade.

The route from Rydal to Ullswater is still more thickly studded with poetic allusions. The *Pass of Kirkstone* is the theme of a characteristic ode; Grisdale Tarn and Helvellyn recur again and again; and Aira Force was one of the spots which the poet best loved to describe, as well as to visit. It was on the shores of Further Gowbarrow that the *Daffodils* danced beneath the trees. These references might be much further multiplied; and the loving diligence of disciples has set before us "the Lake-district as interpreted by Wordsworth" through a multitude of details. But enough has been said to show how completely the poet had absorbed the influences of his dwelling-place; how unique a representative he had become of the lovely district of his birth; how he had made it subject to him by comprehending it, and his own by love.

He visited other countries and described other scenes. Scotland, Wales, Switzerland, France, Germany, Italy, have all a place in his works.

His familiarity with other scenery helped him, doubtless, to a better appreciation of the lake country than he could have gained had he never left it. And, on the other hand, like Caesar in Gaul, or Wellington in the Peninsula, it was because he had so complete a grasp of this chosen base of operations that he was able to come, to see, and to make his own, so swiftly and unfailingly elsewhere. Happy are those whose deep-rooted memories cling like his about some stable home! Whose notion of the world around them has expanded from some prospect of happy tranquillity, instead of being drawn at random from the confusing city's roar! Happier still if that early picture be of one of those rare scenes which have inspired poets and prophets with the retrospective day-dream of a patriarchal, or a golden, age; of some plot of ground like the Ithaca of Odysseus, [Greek: traechsi all agathae koyrotrophos], "rough, but a nurse of *men*;" of some life like that which a poet of kindred spirit to Wordsworth's saw half in vision, half in reality, among the husbandmen of the Italian hills:—

Peace, peace is theirs, and life no fraud that knows,
    Wealth as they will, and when they will, repose;
    On many a hill the happy homesteads stand,
The living lakes through many a vale expand:
Cool glens are there, and shadowy caves divine,
Deep sleep, and far-off voices of the kine;—
From moor to moor the exulting wild deer stray;—
The strenuous youth are strong and sound as they;
One reverence still the untainted race inspires,
God their first thought, and after God their sires;—
These last discerned Astraea's flying hem,
And Virtue's latest footsteps walked with them.

A Chapter from
Wordsworth, 1881

WORDSWORTH.

By John Morley

The poet whose works are contained in the present volume was born in the little town of Cockermouth, in Cumberland, on April 7, 1770. He died at Rydal Mount, in the neighbouring county of Westmoreland, on April 23, 1850. In this long span of mortal years, events of vast and enduring moment shook the world. A handful of scattered and dependent colonies in the northern continent of America made themselves into one of the most powerful and beneficent of states. The ancient monarchy of France, and all the old ordering of which the monarchy had been the keystone, was overthrown, and it was not until after many a violent shock of arms, after terrible slaughter of men, after strange diplomatic combinations, after many social convulsions, after many portentous mutations of empire, that Europe once more settled down for a season into established order and system. In England almost alone, after the loss of her great possessions across the Atlantic Ocean, the fabric of the State stood fast and firm. Yet here, too, in these eighty years, an old order slowly gave place to new. The restoration of peace, after a war conducted with extraordinary tenacity and fortitude, led to a still more wonderful display of ingenuity, industry, and enterprise, in the more fruitful field of commerce and of manufactures. Wealth, in spite of occasional vicissitudes, increased with amazing rapidity. The population of England and Wales grew from being seven and a half millions in 1770, to nearly eighteen millions in 1850. Political power was partially transferred from a territorial aristocracy to the middle and trading classes. Laws were made at once more equal and more humane. During all the tumult of the great war which for so many years bathed Europe in fire, through all the throes and agitations in which peace brought forth the new time, Wordsworth for half a century (1799-1850) dwelt sequestered in unbroken composure and steadfastness in his chosen home amid the mountains and lakes of his native region, working out his own ideal of the high office of the Poet.

The interpretation of life in books and the development of imagination underwent changes of its own. Most of the great lights of the eighteenth century were still burning, though burning low, when Wordsworth came into the world. Pope, indeed, had been dead for six and twenty years, and all the rest of the Queen Anne men had gone. But Gray only died in 1771, and Goldsmith in 1774. Ten years later Johnson's pious and manly heart ceased to beat. Voltaire and Rousseau, those two diverse oracles of their age, both died in 1778. Hume had passed away two years before. Cowper was forty years older than Wordsworth, but Cowper's most delightful work was not produced until 1783. Crabbe, who anticipated Wordsworth's choice of themes from rural life, while treating them with a sterner realism, was virtually his contemporary, having been born in 1754, and dying in 1832. The two great names of his own date were Scott and Coleridge, the first born in 1771, and the second a year afterwards. Then a generation later came another new and illustrious group. Byron was born in 1788, Shelley in 1792, and Keats in 1795. Wordsworth was destined to see one more orb of the first purity and brilliance rise to its place in the poetic firmament. Tennyson's earliest volume of poems was published in 1830, and In Memoriam, one of his two masterpieces, in 1830. Any one who realises for how much these famous names will always stand in the history of human genius, may measure the great transition that Wordsworth's eighty years witnessed in some of men's deepest feelings about art and life and "the speaking face of earth and heaven."

Here, too, Wordsworth stood isolated and apart. Scott and

Southey were valued friends, but, as has been truly said, he thought little of Scott's poetry, and less of Southey's. Of Blake's *Songs of Innocence and Experience* he said, "There is something in the madness of this man which interests me more than the sanity of Lord Byron and Walter Scott." Coleridge was the only member of the shining company with whom he ever had any real intimacy of mind, for whom he ever nourished real deference and admiration as one "unrelentingly possessed by thirst of greatness, love, and beauty," and in whose intellectual power, as the noble lines in the Sixth Book of the *Prelude* so gorgeously attest, he took the passionate interest of a man at once master, disciple, and friend. It is true to say, as Emerson says, that Wordsworth's genius was the great exceptional fact of the literature of his period. But he had no teachers nor inspirers save nature and solitude.

Wordsworth was the son of a solicitor, and all his early circumstances were homely, unpretentious, and rather straitened. His mother died when he was eight years old, and when his father followed her five years later, two of his uncles provided means for continuing at Cambridge the education which had been begun in the rural grammar-school of Hawkshead. It was in 1787 that he went up to St. John's College. He took his Bachelor's degree at the beginning of 1791, and there his connection with the university ended.

For some years after leaving Cambridge, Wordsworth let himself drift. He did not feel good enough for the Church; he shrank from the law; fancying that he had talents for command, he thought of being a soldier. Meanwhile, he passed a short time desultorily in London. Towards the end of 1791, through Paris, he passed on to Orleans and Blois, where he made some friends and spent most of a year. He returned to Paris in October 1792. France was no longer standing on the top of golden hours. The September massacres filled the sky with a lurid flame. Wordsworth still retained his ardent faith in the Revolution, and was even ready, though no better than "a landsman on the deck of a ship struggling with a hideous storm," to make common cause with the Girondists. But the prudence of friends at home forced him back to England before the beginning of the terrible year of '93. With his return closed that first survey of its inheritance, which most serious souls are wont to make in the fervid prime of early manhood.

It would be idle to attempt any commentary on the bare facts that we have just recapitulated; for Wordsworth himself has clothed them with their full force and meaning in the *Prelude*. This record of the growth of a poet's mind, told by the poet himself with all the sincerity of which he was capable, is never likely to be popular. Of that, as of so much more of his poetry, we must say that, as a whole, it has not the musical, harmonious, sympathetic quality which seizes us in even the prose of such a book as Rousseau's *Confessions*. Macaulay thought the *Prelude* a poorer and more tiresome *Excursion*, with the old flimsy philosophy about the effect of scenery on the mind, the old crazy mystical metaphysics, and the endless wilderness of twaddle; still he admits that there are some fine descriptions and energetic declamations. All Macaulay's tastes and habits of mind made him a poor judge of such a poet as Wordsworth. He valued spirit, energy, pomp, stateliness of form and diction, and actually thought Dryden's fine lines about to-morrow being falser than the former clay equal to any eight lines in Lucretius. But his words truly express the effect of the *Prelude* on more vulgar minds than his own. George Eliot, on the other hand, who had the inward eye that was not among Macaulay's gifts, found the *Prelude* full of material for a daily liturgy, and it is easy to imagine how she fondly lingered, as she did, over such a thought as this—

"There is
One great society alone on earth:
The noble Living and the noble Dead."

102

There is, too, as may be found imbedded even in Wordsworth's dullest work, many a line of the truest poetical quality, such as that on Newton's statue in the silent Chapel of Trinity College—

"The marble index of a mind for ever
Voyaging through strange seas of Thought alone."

Apart, however, from beautiful lines like this, and from many noble passages of high reflection set to sonorous verse, this remarkable poem is in its whole effect unique in impressive power, as a picture of the advance of an elect and serious spirit from childhood and school-time, through the ordeal of adolescence, through close contact with stirring and enormous events, to that decisive stage when it has found the sources of its strength, and is fully and finally prepared to put its temper to the proof. The three Books that describe the poet's residence in France have a special and a striking value of their own. Their presentation of the phases of good men's minds as the successive scenes of the Revolution unfolded themselves has real historic interest. More than this, it is an abiding lesson to brave men how to bear themselves in hours of public stress. It portrays exactly that mixture of persevering faith and hope with firm and reasoned judgment, with which I like to think that Turgot, if he had lived, would have confronted the workings of the Revolutionary power. Great masters in many kinds have been inspired by the French Revolution. Human genius might seem to have exhausted itself in the burning political passion of Burke, in the glowing melodrama of fire and tears of Carlyle, Michelet, Hugo; but the ninth, tenth, and eleventh Books of the *Prelude*, by their strenuous simplicity, their deep truthfulness, their slowfooted and inexorable transition from ardent hope to dark imaginations, sense of woes to come, sorrow for human kind, and pain of heart, breathe the very spirit of the great catastrophe. There is none of the ephemeral glow of the political exhortation, none of the tiresome falsity of the dithyramb in history.

Wordsworth might well wish that some dramatic tale, endued with livelier shapes and flinging out less guarded words, might set forth the lessons of his experience. The material was fitting. The story of these three Books has something of the severity, the self-control, the inexorable necessity of classic tragedy, and like classic tragedy it has a noble end. The dregs and sour sediment that reaction from exaggerated hope is so apt to stir in poor natures had no place here. The French Revolution made the one crisis in Wordsworth's mental history, the one heavy assault on his continence of soul, and when he emerged from it all his greatness remained to him. After a long spell of depression, bewilderment, mortification, and sore disappointment, the old faith in new shapes was given back.

> "Nature's self,
> By all varieties of human love
> Assisted, led me back through opening day
> To those sweet counsels between head and heart
> Whence grew that genuine knowledge, fraught with peace,
> Which, through the later sinkings of this cause,
> Hath still upheld me and upholds me now."

It was six years after his return from France before Wordsworth finally settled down in the scenes with which his name and the power of his genius were to be for ever associated. During this interval it was that two great sources of personal influence were opened to him. He entered upon that close and beloved companionship with his sister, which remained unbroken to the end of their days; and he first made the acquaintance of Coleridge. The character of Dorothy Wordsworth has long taken its place in the gallery of admirable and devoted women who have inspired the work and the thoughts of great men. "She is a woman, indeed," said Coleridge, "in mind I mean, and heart; for her person is such that if you expected to see a pretty woman, you would think her rather ordinary; if you expected to see an ordinary woman, you would think her pretty." To the solidity, sense, and strong intelligence of the Wordsworth stock she added a grace, a warmth, a liveliness peculiarly her own. Her nature shines transparent in her letters, in her truly admirable journal, and in every report that we have of her. Wordsworth's own feelings for her, and his sense of the debt that he owed to her faithful affection and eager mind, he has placed on lasting record.

The intimacy with Coleridge was, as has been said, Wordsworth's one strong friendship, and must be counted among the highest examples of that generous relation between great writers. Unlike in the quality of their genius, and unlike in force of character and the fortunes of life, they remained bound to one another by sympathies that neither time nor harsh trial ever extinguished. Coleridge had left Cambridge in 1794, had married, had started various unsuccessful projects for combining the improvement of mankind with the earning of an income, and was now settled in a small cottage at Nether Stowey, in Somersetshire, with an acre and a half of land, from which he hoped to raise corn and vegetables enough to support himself and his wife, as well as to feed a couple of pigs on the refuse. Wordsworth and his sister were settled at Racedown, near Crewkerne, in Dorsetshire. In 1797 they moved to Alfoxden, in Somersetshire, their principal inducement to the change being Coleridge's society. The friendship bore fruit in the production of *Lyrical Ballads* in 1798, mainly the work of Wordsworth, but containing no less notable a contribution from Coleridge than the *Ancient Mariner.* The two poets only received thirty guineas for their work, and the publisher lost his money. The taste of the country was not yet ripe for Wordsworth's poetic experiment.

Immediately after the publication of the *Lyrical Ballads*, the two Wordsworths and Coleridge started from Yarmouth for Hamburg. Coleridge's account in Satyrane's Letters, published In the *Biographia Literaria*, of the voyage and of the conversation between the two English poets and Klopstock, is worth turning to. The pastor told them that Klopstock was the German Milton. "A very German Milton indeed," they thought. The Wordsworths remained for four wintry months at Goslar, in Saxony, while Coleridge went on to Ratzeburg, Göttingen, and other places, mastering German, and "delving in the unwholesome quicksilver mines of metaphysic depths." Wordsworth made little way with the language, but worked diligently at his own verse.

When they came back to England, Wordsworth and his sister found their hearts turning with irresistible attraction to their own familiar countryside. They at last made their way to Grasmere. The opening book of the *Recluse*, which is published for the first time in the present volume, describes in fine verse the emotions and the scene. The face of this delicious vale is not quite what it was when

> "Cottages of mountain stone
> Clustered like stars some few, but single most,
> And lurking dimly in their shy retreats,
> Or glancing at each other cheerful looks
> Like separated stars with clouds between."

But it is foolish to let ourselves be fretted by the villa, the hotel, and the tourist. We may well be above all this in a scene that is haunted by a great poetic shade.

The substantial features and elements of beauty still remain, the crags and woody steeps, the lake, "its one green island and its winding shores; the multitude of little rocky hills." Wordsworth was not the first poet to feel its fascination. Gray visited the Lakes in the autumn of 1769, and coming into the vale of Grasmere from the north-west, declared it to be one of the sweetest landscapes that art ever attempted to imitate, an unsuspected paradise of peace and rusticity.

We cannot indeed compare the little crystal mere, set like a gem in the verdant circle of the hills, with the grandeur and glory of Lucerne, or the radiant gladness and expanse of Como: yet it has an inspiration of its own, to delight, to soothe, to fortify, and to refresh.

> "What want we? have we not perpetual streams,
> Warm woods, and sunny hills, and fresh green fields,
> And mountains not less green, and flocks and herds,
> And thickets full of songsters, and the voice
> Of lordly birds, an unexpected sound
> Heard now and then from morn to latest eve,
> Admonishing the man who walks below
> Of solitude and silence in the sky.
> These have we, and a thousand nooks of earth
> Have also these, but nowhere else is found,
> Nowhere (or is it fancy?) can be found
> The one sensation that is here;...'tis the sense
> Of majesty, and beauty, and repose,
> A blended holiness of earth and sky,
> Something that makes this individual spot,
> This small abiding-place of many men,
> A termination, and a last retreat,
> A centre, come from wheresoe'er you will,
> A whole without dependence or defect,
> Made for itself, and happy in itself,
> Perfect contentment, Unity entire."

In the Grasmere vale Wordsworth lived for half a century, first in a little cottage at the northern corner of the lake, and then (1813) in a more commodious house at Rydal Mount at the southern end, on the road to Ambleside. In 1802 he married Mary Hutchinson, of Penrith, and this completed the circle of his felicity. Mary, he once said, was to his ear the most musical and most truly English in sound of all the names we have. The name was of harmonious omen. The two beautiful sonnets that he wrote on his wife's portrait long years after, when "morning into noon had passed, noon into eve," show how much her large heart and humble mind had done for the blessedness of his home.

Their life was almost more simple than that of the dalesmen their neighbours. "It is my opinion," ran one of his oracular sayings to Sir George Beaumont, "that a man of letters, and indeed all public men of every pursuit, should be severely frugal." Means were found for supporting the modest home out of two or three small windfalls bequeathed by friends or relatives, and by the time that children had begun to come Wordsworth was raised to affluence by obtaining the post of distributor of stamps for Westmoreland and part of Cumberland. His life was happily devoid of striking external incident. Its essential part lay in meditation and composition.

He was surrounded by friends. Southey had made a home for himself and his beloved library a few miles over the hills, at Keswick. De Quincey, with his clever brains and shallow character, took up his abode in the cottage which Wordsworth had first lived in at Grasmere. Coleridge, born the most golden genius of them all, came to and fro in those fruitless unhappy wanderings which consumed a life that once promised to be so rich in blessing and in glory. In later years Dr. Arnold built a house at Fox How, attracted by the Wordsworths and the scenery; and other lesser lights came into the neighbourhood. "Our intercourse with the Wordsworths," Arnold wrote on the occasion of his first visit in 1832, "was one of the brightest spots of all; nothing could exceed their friendliness, and my almost daily walks with him were things not to be forgotten. Once and once only we had a good fight about the Reform Bill during a walk up Greenhead Ghyll to see the unfinished sheep-fold, recorded in *Michael*. But I am sure that our political disagreement did not at all interfere with our enjoyment of each other's society; for I think that in the great principles of things we agreed very entirely." It ought to be possible, for that matter, for magnanimous men, even if they do not agree in the great principles of things, to keep pleasant terms with one another for more than one afternoon's walk. Many pilgrims came, and the poet seems to have received them with cheerful equanimity. Emerson called upon him in 1833, and found him plain, elderly, whitehaired, not prepossessing. "He led me out into his garden, and showed me the gravel walk in which thousands of his lines were composed. He had just returned from Staffa, and within three days had made three sonnets on Fingal's Cave, and was composing a fourth when he was called in to see me. He said, 'If you are interested in my verses, perhaps you will like to hear these lines.' I gladly assented, and he recollected himself for a few moments, and then stood forth and repeated, one after the other, the three entire sonnets with great animation. This recitation was so unlooked for and surprising—he, the old Wordsworth, standing apart, and reciting to me in a garden-walk, like a schoolboy declaiming—that I at first was near to laugh; but recollecting myself, that I had come thus far to see a poet, and he was chanting poems to me, I saw that he was right and I was wrong, and gladly gave myself up to hear. He never was in haste to publish; partly because he corrected a good deal…. He preferred such of his poems as touched the affections to any others; for whatever is didactic—what theories of society, and so on—might perish quickly, but whatever combined a truth with an affection was good to-day and good for ever" (*English Traits*, ch. i.).

Wordsworth was far too wise to encourage the pilgrims to turn into abiding sojourners in his chosen land. Clough has described how, when he was a lad of eighteen (1837), with a mild surprise he heard the venerable poet correct the tendency to exaggerate the importance of flowers and fields, lakes, waterfalls, and scenery. "People come to the Lakes," said Wordsworth, "and are charmed with a particular spot, and build a house, and find themselves discontented, forgetting that these things are only the sauce and garnish of life."

In spite of a certain hardness and stiffness, Wordsworth must have been an admirable companion for anybody capable of true elevation of mind. The unfortunate Haydon says, with his usual accent of enthusiasm, after a saunter at Hampstead, "Never did any man so beguile the time as Wordsworth. His purity of heart, his kindness, his soundness of principle, his information, his knowledge, and the intense and eager feelings with which he pours forth all he knows, affect, interest, and enchant one" (*Autobiog.* i. 298, 384). The diary of Crabb Robinson, the correspondence of Charles Lamb, the delightful autobiography of Mrs. Fletcher, and much less delightfully the autobiography of Harriet Martineau, all help us to realise by many a trait Wordsworth's daily walk and conversation. Of all the glimpses that we get, from these and many other sources, none are more pleasing than those of the intercourse between Wordsworth and Scott. They were the two manliest and most wholesome men of genius of their time. They held different theories of poetic art, but their affection and esteem for one another never varied, from the early days when Scott and his young wife visited Wordsworth in his cottage at Grasmere, down to that sorrowful autumn evening (1831) when Wordsworth and his daughter went to Abbotsford to bid farewell to the wondrous potentate, then just about to start on his vain search for new life, followed by "the might of the whole earth's good wishes."

Of Wordsworth's demeanour and physical presence, De Quincey's account, silly, coxcombical, and vulgar, is the worst; Carlyle's, as might be expected from his magical gift of portraiture, is the best. Carlyle cared little for Wordsworth's poetry, had a real respect for the antique greatness of his devotion to Poverty and Peasanthood, recognised his strong intellectual powers and strong character, but thought him rather dull, bad-tempered, unproductive, and almost wearisome, and found his divine reflections and unfathomabilities stinted, scanty, uncertain, palish. From these and many other disparagements, one gladly passes to the picture of the poet as he was in the flesh at a breakfast-party given by Henry Taylor, at a tavern in St. James's Street, in 1840. The subject of the talk was Literature, its laws, practices, and observances:—"He talked well in his way; with veracity, easy brevity and force; as a wise tradesman would of his tools and workshop, and as no unwise one could. His voice was good, frank, and sonorous, though practically clear, distinct, and forcible, rather than melodious; the tone of him business-like, sedately confident; no discourtesy, yet no anxiety about being courteous: a fine wholesome rusticity, fresh as his mountain breezes, sat well on the stalwart veteran, and on all he said and did. You would have said he was a usually taciturn man, glad to unlock himself to audience sympathetic and intelligent, when such offered itself. His face bore marks of much, not always peaceful, meditation; the look of it not bland or benevolent, so much as close, impregnable, and hard; a man *multa tacere loquive paratus*, in a world where he had experienced no lack of contradictions as he strode along! The eyes were not very brilliant, but they had a quiet clearness; there was enough of brow, and well shaped; rather too much of cheek ('horse-face,' I have heard satirists say), face of squarish shape and decidedly longish, as I think the head itself was (its 'length' going horizontal); he was large-boned, lean, but still firm-knit, tall, and strong-looking when he stood; a right good old steel-gray figure, with rustic simplicity and dignity about him, and a vivacious *strength* looking through him which might have suited one of those old steel-gray *Markgrafs* [Graf = *Grau*,'Steel-gray'] whom Henry the Fowler set up to ward the 'marches,' and do battle with the intrusive heathen, in a stalwart and judicious manner."

Whoever might be his friends within an easy walk, or dwelling afar, the poet knew how to live his own life. The three fine sonnets headed *Personal Talk*, so well known, so warmly accepted in our better hours, so easily forgotten in hours not so good between pleasant levities and grinding preoccupations, show us how little his neighbours had to do with the poet's genial seasons of "smooth passions, smooth discourse, and joyous thought."

For those days Wordsworth was a considerable traveller. Between 1820 and 1837 he made long tours abroad, to Switzerland, to Holland, to Belgium, to Italy. In other years he visited Wales, Scotland, and Ireland. He was no mechanical tourist, admiring to order and marvelling by regulation; and he confessed to Mrs. Fletcher that he fell asleep before the Venus de Medici at Florence. But the product of these wanderings is to be seen in some of his best sonnets, such as the first on Calais Beach, the famous one on Westminster Bridge, the second of the two on Bruges, where "the Spirit of Antiquity mounts to the seat of grace within the mind—a deeper peace than that in deserts found"—and in some other fine pieces.

In weightier matters than mere travel, Wordsworth showed himself no mere recluse. He watched the great affairs then being transacted in Europe with the ardent interest of his youth, and his sonnets to Liberty, commemorating the attack by France upon the Swiss, the fate of Venice, the struggle of Hofer, the resistance of Spain, give no unworthy expression to some of the best of the many and varied motives that animated England in her long struggle with Bonaparte. The sonnet to Toussaint l'Ouverture concludes with some of the noblest lines in the English language. The strong verses on the expected death of Mr. Fox are alive with a magnanimous public spirit that goes deeper than the accidents of political opinion. In his young days he had sent Fox a copy of the *Lyrical Ballads*, with a long letter indicating his sense of Fox's great and generous qualities. Pitt he admits that he could never regard with complacency. "I believe him, however," he said, "to have been as disinterested a man, and as true a lover of his country, as it was possible for so ambitious a man to be. His first wish (though probably unknown to himself) was that his country should prosper under his administration; his next that it should prosper. Could the order of these wishes have been reversed, Mr. Pitt would have avoided many of the grievous mistakes into which, I think, he fell." "You always went away from Burke," he once told Haydon, "with your mind filled; from Fox with your feelings excited; and from Pitt with wonder at his having had the power to make the worse appear the better reason."

112

Of the poems composed under the influence of that best kind of patriotism which ennobles local attachments by associating them with the lasting elements of moral grandeur and heroism it is needless to speak. They have long taken their place as something higher even than literary classics. As years began to dull the old penetration of a mind which had once approached, like other youths, the shield of human nature from the golden side, and had been eager to "clear a passage for just government," Wordsworth lost his interest in progress. Waterloo may be taken for the date at which his social grasp began to fail, and with it his poetic glow. He opposed Catholic emancipation as stubbornly as Eldon, and the Reform Bill as bitterly as Croker. For the practical reforms of his day, even in education, for which he had always spoken up, Wordsworth was not a force. His heart clung to England as he found it. "This concrete attachment to the scenes about him," says Mr. Myers, "had always formed an important element In his character. Ideal politics, whether in Church or State, had never occupied his mind, which sought rather to find its informing principles embodied in the England of his own day." This flowed, we may suppose, from Burke. In a passage in the seventh Book of the *Prelude*, he describes, in lines a little prosaic but quite true, how he sat, saw, and heard, not unthankful nor uninspired, the great orator

"While he forewarns, denounces, launches forth
Against all systems built on abstract rights."

The Church, as conceived by the spirit of Laud, and described by Hooker's voice, was the great symbol of the union of high and stable institution with thought, faith, right living, and "sacred religion, mother of form and fear." As might be expected from such a point of view, the church pieces, to which Wordsworth gave so much thought, are, with few exceptions, such as the sonnet on *Seathwaite Chapel*, formal, hard, and very thinly enriched with spiritual graces or unction. They are ecclesiastical, not religious. In religious poetry, the Church of England finds her most affecting voice, not in Wordsworth, but in the *Lyra Innocentium* and the *Christian Year*. Wordsworth abounds in the true devotional cast of mind, but less than anywhere else does it show in his properly ecclesiastical verse.

It was perhaps natural that when events no longer inspired him, Wordsworth should have turned with new feelings towards the classic, and discovered a virtue in classic form to which his own method had hitherto made him a little blind. Towards the date of Waterloo, he read over again some of the Latin writers, in attempting to prepare his son for college. He even at a later date set about a translation of the *Aeneid* of Virgil, but the one permanent result of the classic movement in his mind is *Laodamia*. Earlier in life he had translated some books of Ariosto at the rate of a hundred lines a day, and he even attempted fifteen of the sonnets of Michael Angelo, but so much meaning is compressed into so little room in those pieces that he found the difficulty insurmountable. He had a high opinion of the resources of the Italian language. The poetry of Dante and of Michael Angelo, he said, proves that if there be little majesty and strength in Italian verse, the fault is in the authors and not in the tongue.

Our last glimpse of Wordsworth in the full and peculiar power of his genius is the Ode *Composed on an evening of extraordinary splendour and beauty*. It is the one exception to the critical dictum that all his good work was done in the decade between 1798 and 1808. He lived for more than thirty years after this fine composition. But he added nothing more of value to the work that he had already done. The public appreciation of it was very slow. The most influential among the critics were for long hostile and contemptuous. Never at any time did Wordsworth come near to such popularity as that of Scott or of Byron. Nor was this all. For many years most readers of poetry thought more even of *Lalla Rookh* than of the *Excursion*. While Scott, Byron, and Moore were receiving thousands of pounds, Wordsworth received nothing. Between 1830 and 1840 the current turned in Wordsworth's direction, and when he received the honour of a doctor's degree at the Oxford Commemoration in 1839, the Sheldonian theatre made him the hero of the day. In the spring of 1843 Southey died, and Sir Robert Peel pressed Wordsworth to succeed him in the office of Poet-Laureate. "It is a tribute of respect," said the Minister, "justly due to the first of living poets." But almost immediately the light of his common popularity was eclipsed by Tennyson, as it had earlier been eclipsed by Scott, by Byron, and in some degree by Shelley. Yet his fame among those who know, among competent critics with a right to judge, to-day stands higher than it ever stood. Only two writers have contributed so many lines of daily popularity and application. In the handbooks of familiar quotations Wordsworth fills more space than anybody save Shakespeare and Pope. He exerted commanding influence over great minds that have powerfully affected our generation. "I never before," said George Eliot in the days when her character was forming itself (1839), "met with so many of my own feelings expressed just as I should like them," and her reverence for Wordsworth remained to the end. J.S. Mill has described how important an event in his life was his first reading of Wordsworth. "What made his poems a medicine for my state of mind was that they expressed not mere outward beauty, but states of feeling and of thought coloured by feeling, under the excitement of beauty. I needed to be made to feel that there was real permanent happiness in tranquil contemplation. Wordsworth taught me this, not only without turning away from, but with greatly increased interest in the common feelings and common destiny of human beings" (*Autobiog.*, 148). This effect of Wordsworth on Mill is the very illustration of the phrase of a later poet of our own day, one of the most eminent and by his friends best beloved of all those whom Wordsworth had known, and on whom he poured out a generous portion of his own best spirit:—

Time may restore us in his course
Goethe's sage mind and Byron's force.
But where will Europe's latter hour
Again find Wordsworth's healing power?

It is the power for which Matthew Arnold found this happy designation that compensates us for that absence of excitement of which the heedless complain in Wordsworth's verse— excitement so often meaning mental fever, hysterics, distorted passion, or other fitful agitation of the soul.

Pretensions are sometimes advanced as to Wordsworth's historic position, which involve a mistaken view of literary history. Thus, we are gravely told by the too zealous Wordsworthian that the so-called poets of the eighteenth century were simply men of letters; they had various accomplishments and great general ability, but their thoughts were expressed in prose, or in mere metrical diction, which passed current as poetry without being so. Yet Burns belonged wholly to the eighteenth century (1759-96), and no verse-writer is so little literary as Burns, so little prosaic; no writer more truly poetic in melody, diction, thought, feeling, and spontaneous song. It was Burns who showed Wordsworth's own youth "How verse may build a princely throne on humble truth." Nor can we understand how Cowper is to be set down as simply a man of letters. We may, too, if we please, deny the name of poetry to Collins's tender and pensive *Ode to Evening*; but we can only do this on critical principles, which would end in classing the author of *Lycidas* and *Comus*, of the *Allegro* and *Penseroso*, as a writer of various accomplishments and great general ability, but at bottom simply a man of letters and by no means a poet. It is to Gray, however, that we must turn for the distinctive character of the best poetry of the eighteenth century. With reluctance we will surrender the Pindaric Odes, though not without risking the observation that some of Wordsworth's own criticism on Gray is as narrow and as much beside the mark as Jeffrey's on the *Excursion*. But the *Ode on Eton College* is not to have grudged to it the noble name and true quality of poetry, merely because, as one of Johnson's most unfortunate criticisms expresses it, the ode suggests nothing to Gray which every beholder does not equally think and feel. To find beautiful and pathetic language, set to harmonious numbers, for the common impressions of meditative minds, is no small part of the poet's task. That part has never been achieved by any poet in any tongue with more complete perfection and success than in the immortal *Elegy*, of which we may truly say that it has for nearly a century and a half given to greater multitudes of men more of the exquisite pleasure of poetry than any other single piece in all the glorious treasury of English verse. It abounds, as Johnson says, "with images which find a mirror in every mind, and with sentiments to which every bosom returns an echo." These moving commonplaces of the human lot Gray approached through books and studious contemplation; not, as Wordsworth approached them, by daily contact with the lives and habit of men and the forces and magical apparitions of external nature. But it is a narrow view to suppose that the men of the eighteenth century did not look through the literary conventions of the day to the truths of life and nature behind them. The conventions have gone, or are changed, and we are all glad of it. Wordsworth effected a wholesome deliverance when he attacked the artificial diction, the personifications, the allegories, the antitheses, the barren rhymes and monotonous metres, which the reigning taste had approved. But while welcoming the new freshness, sincerity, and direct and fertile return on nature, that is a very bad reason why we should disparage poetry so genial, so simple, so humane, and so perpetually pleasing, as the best verse of the rationalistic century.

What Wordsworth did was to deal with themes that had been partially handled by precursors and contemporaries, in a larger and more devoted spirit, with wider amplitude of illustration, and with the steadfastness and persistency of a religious teacher. "Every great poet is a teacher," he said; "I wish to be considered as a teacher or as nothing." It may be doubted whether his general proposition is at all true, and whether it is any more the essential business of a poet to be a teacher than it was the business of Handel, Beethoven, or Mozart. They attune the soul to high states of feeling; the direct lesson is often as nought. But of himself no view could be more sound. He is a teacher, or he is nothing. "To console the afflicted; to add sunshine to daylight by making the happy happier; to teach the young and the gracious of every age to see, to think, and feel, and therefore to become more actively and sincerely virtuous"—that was his vocation; to show that the mutual adaptation of the external world and the inner mind is able to shape a paradise from the "simple produce of the common day"—that was his high argument.

Simplification was, as I have said elsewhere, the keynote of the revolutionary time. Wordsworth was its purest exponent, but he had one remarkable peculiarity, which made him, in England at least, not only its purest but its greatest. While leading men to pierce below the artificial and conventional to the natural man and natural life, as Rousseau did, Wordsworth still cherished the symbols, the traditions, and the great institutes of social order. Simplification of life and thought and feeling was to be accomplished without summoning up the dangerous spirit of destruction and revolt. Wordsworth lived with nature, yet waged no angry railing war against society. The chief opposing force to Wordsworth in literature was Byron. Whatever he was in his heart, Byron in his work was drawn by all the forces of his character, genius, and circumstances to the side of violent social change, and hence the extraordinary popularity of Byron in the continental camp of emancipation. Communion with nature is in Wordsworth's doctrine the school of duty. With Byron nature is the mighty consoler and the vindicator of the rebel.

A curious thing, which we may note in passing, is that Wordsworth, who clung fervently to the historic foundations of society as it stands, was wholly indifferent to history; while Byron, on the contrary, as the fourth canto of *Childe Harold* is enough to show, had at least the sentiment of history in as great a degree as any poet that ever lived, and has given to it by far the most magnificent expression. No doubt, it was history on its romantic, rather than its philosophic or its political side.

On Wordsworth's exact position in the hierarchy of sovereign poets, a deep difference of estimate still divides even the most excellent judges. Nobody now dreams of placing him so low as the *Edinburgh Reviewers* did, nor so high as Southey placed him when he wrote to the author of *Philip van Artevelde* in 1829 that a greater poet than Wordsworth there never has been nor ever will be. An extravagance of this kind was only the outburst of generous friendship. Coleridge deliberately placed Wordsworth "nearest of all modern writers to Shakespeare and Milton, yet in a kind perfectly unborrowed and his own." Arnold, himself a poet of rare and memorable quality, declares his firm belief that the poetical performance of Wordsworth is, after that of Shakespeare and Milton, undoubtedly the most considerable in our language from the Elizabethan age to the present time. Dryden, Pope, Gray, Cowper, Goldsmith, Burns, Coleridge, Byron, Shelley, Keats—"Wordsworth's name deserves to stand, and will finally stand, above them all." Mr. Myers, also a poet, and the author of a volume on Wordsworth as much distinguished by insight as by admirable literary grace and power, talks of "a Plato, a Dante, a Wordsworth," all three in a breath, as stars of equal magnitude in the great spiritual firmament. To Mr. Swinburne, on the contrary, all these panegyrical estimates savour of monstrous and intolerable exaggeration. Amid these contentions of celestial minds it will be safest to content ourselves with one or two plain observations in the humble positive degree, without hurrying into high and final comparatives and superlatives.

One admission is generally made at the outset. Whatever definition of poetry we fix upon, whether that it is the language of passion or imagination formed into regular numbers; or, with Milton, that it should be "simple, sensuous, impassioned;" in any case there are great tracts in Wordsworth which, by no definition and on no terms, can be called poetry. If we say with Shelley, that poetry is what redeems from decay the visitations of the divinity in man, and is the record of the best and happiest moments of the best and happiest minds, then are we bound to agree that Wordsworth records too many moments that are not specially good or happy, that he redeems from decay frequent visitations that are not from any particular divinity in man, and treats them all as very much on a level. Mr. Arnold is undoubtedly right in his view that, to be receivable as a classic, Wordsworth must be relieved of a great deal of the poetical baggage that now encumbers him.

The faults and hindrances in Wordsworth's poetry are obvious to every reader. For one thing, the intention to instruct, to improve the occasion, is too deliberate and too hardly pressed. "We hate poetry," said Keats, "that has a palpable design upon us. Poetry should be great and unobtrusive." Charles Lamb's friendly remonstrance on one of Wordsworth's poems is applicable to more of them: "The instructions conveyed in it are too direct; they don't slide into the mind of the reader while he is imagining no such matter."

Then, except the sonnets and half a score of the pieces where he reaches his topmost height, there are few of his poems that are not too long, and it often happens even that no degree of reverence for the teacher prevents one from finding passages of almost unbearable prolixity. A defence was once made by a great artist for what, to the unregenerate mind, seemed the merciless tardiness of movement in one of Goethe's romances, that it was meant to impress on his readers the slow march and the tedium of events in human life. The lenient reader may give Wordsworth the advantage of the same ingenious explanation. We may venture on a counsel which is more to the point, in warning the student that not seldom in these blocks of afflicting prose, suddenly we come upon some of the profoundest and most beautiful passages that the poet ever wrote. In deserts of preaching we find, almost within sight of one another, delightful oases of purest poetry.

Besides being prolix, Wordsworth is often cumbrous; has often no flight; is not liquid, is not musical. He is heavy and self-conscious with the burden of his message. How much at his best he is, when, as in the admirable and truly Wordsworthian poem of *Michael*, he spares us a sermon and leaves us the story. Then, he is apt to wear a somewhat stiff-cut garment of solemnity, when not solemnity, but either sternness or sadness, which are so different things, would seem the fitter mood. In truth Wordsworth hardly knows how to be stern, as Dante or Milton was stern; nor has he the note of plangent sadness which strikes the ear in men as morally inferior to him as Rousseau, Keats, Shelley, or Coleridge; nor has he the Olympian air with which Goethe delivered sage oracles. This mere solemnity is specially oppressive in some parts of the *Excursion*—the performance where we best see the whole poet, and where the poet most absolutely identifies himself with his subject. Yet, even in the midst of these solemn discoursings, he suddenly introduces an episode in which his peculiar power is at its height. There is no better instance of this than the passage in the second Book of the *Excursion*, where he describes with a fidelity, at once realistic and poetic, the worn-out almsman, his patient life and sorry death, and then the unimaginable vision in the skies, as they brought the ancient man down through dull mists from the mountain ridge to die. These hundred and seventy lines are like the landscape in which they were composed; you can no more appreciate the beauty of the one by a single or a second perusal, than you can the other in a scamper through the vale on the box of the coach. But any lover of poetry who will submit himself with leisure and meditation to the impressions of the story, the pity of it, the naturalness of it, the glory and the mystic splendours of the indifferent heavens, will feel that here indeed is the true strength which out of the trivial raises expression for the pathetic and the sublime.

Apart, however, from excess of prolixity and of solemnity, can it be really contended that in purely poetic quality—in aerial freedom and space, in radiant purity of light or depth and variety of colour, in penetrating and subtle sweetness of music, in supple mastery of the instrument, in vivid spontaneity of imagination, in clean-cut sureness of touch—Wordsworth is not surpassed by men who were below him in weight and greatness? Even in his own field of the simple and the pastoral has he touched so sweet and spontaneous a note as Burns's *Daisy*, or the *Mouse*? When men seek immersion or absorption in the atmosphere of pure poesy, without lesson or moral, or anything but delight of fancy and stir of imagination, they will find him less congenial to their mood than poets not worthy to loose the latchet of his shoe in the greater elements of his art. In all these comparisons, it is not merely Wordsworth's theme and motive and dominant note that are different; the skill of hand is different, and the musical ear and the imaginative eye.

To maintain or to admit so much as this, however, is not to say the last word. The question is whether Wordsworth, however unequal to Shelley in lyric quality, to Coleridge or to Keats in imaginative quality, to Burns in tenderness, warmth, and that humour which is so nearly akin to pathos, to Byron in vividness and energy, yet possesses excellences of his own which place him in other respects above these master-spirits of his time. If the question is to be answered affirmatively, it is clear that only in one direction must we look. The trait that really places Wordsworth on an eminence above his poetic contemporaries, and ranks him, as the ages are likely to rank him, on a line just short of the greatest of all time, is his direct appeal to will and conduct. "There is volition and self-government in every line of his poetry, and his best thoughts come from his steady resistance to the ebb and flow of ordinary desires and regrets. He contests the ground inch by inch with all despondent and indolent humours, and often, too, with movements of inconsiderate and wasteful joy" (*R.H. Hutton*). That would seem to be his true distinction and superiority over men to whom more had been given of fire, passion, and ravishing music. Those who deem the end of poetry to be intoxication, fever, or rainbow dreams, can care little for

Wordsworth. If its end be not intoxication, but on the contrary a search from the wide regions of imagination and feeling for elements of composure deep and pure, and of self-government in a far loftier sense than the merely prudential, then Wordsworth has a gift of his own in which he was approached by no poet of his time. Scott's sane and humane genius, with much the same aims, yet worked with different methods. He once remonstrated with Lockhart for being too apt to measure things by some reference to literature. "I have read books enough," said Scott, "and observed and conversed with enough of eminent and splendidly cultivated minds; but I assure you, I have heard higher sentiments from the lips of poor uneducated men and women, when exerting the spirit of severe yet gentle heroism under difficulties and afflictions, or speaking their simple thoughts as to circumstances in the lot of friends and neighbours, than I ever yet met with out of the pages of the Bible. We shall never learn to respect our real calling and destiny, unless we have taught ourselves to consider everything as moonshine compared with the education of the heart." This admirable deliverance of Scott's is, so far as it goes, eminently Wordsworthian; but Wordsworth went higher and further, striving not only to move the sympathies of the heart, but to enlarge the understanding, and exalt and widen the spiritual vision, all with the aim of leading us towards firmer and austerer self-control.

Certain favourers of Wordsworth answer our question with a triumphant affirmative, on the strength of some ethical, or metaphysical, or theological system which they believe themselves to find in him. But is it credible that poets can permanently live by systems? Or is not system, whether ethical, theological, or philosophical, the heavy lead of poetry? Lucretius is indisputably one of the mighty poets of the world, but Epicureanism is not the soul of that majestic muse. So with Wordsworth. Thought is, on the whole, predominant over feeling in his verse, but a prevailing atmosphere of deep and solemn reflection does not make a system. His theology and his ethics, and his so-called Platonical metaphysics, have as little to do with the power of his poetry over us, as the imputed Arianism or any other aspect of the theology of *Paradise Lost* has to do with the strength and the sublimity of Milton, and his claim to a high perpetual place in the hearts of men. It is best to be entirely sceptical as to the existence of system and ordered philosophy in Wordsworth. When he tells us that "one impulse from a vernal wood may teach you more of man, of moral evil and of good, than all the sages can," such a proposition cannot be seriously taken as more than a half-playful sally for the benefit of some too bookish friend. No impulse from a vernal wood can teach us anything at all of moral evil and of good. When he says that it is his faith, "that every flower enjoys the air it breathes," and that when the budding twigs spread out their fan to catch the air, he is compelled to think "that there was pleasure there," he expresses a charming poetic fancy and no more, and it is idle to pretend to see in it the fountain of a system of philosophy. In the famous *Ode on Intimations of Immortality*, the poet doubtless does point to a set of philosophic ideas, more or less complete; but the thought from which he sets out, that our birth is but a sleep and a forgetting, and that we are less and less able to perceive the visionary gleam, less and less alive to the glory and the dream of external nature, as infancy recedes further from us, is, with all respect for the declaration of Mr. Ruskin to the contrary, contrary to notorious fact, experience, and truth. It is a beggarly conception, no doubt, to judge as if poetry should always be capable of a prose rendering; but it is at least fatal to the philosophic pretension of a line or a stanza if, when it is fairly reduced to prose, the prose discloses that it is nonsense, and there is at least one stanza of the great *Ode* that this doom would assuredly await. Wordsworth's claim, his special gift, his lasting contribution, lies in the extraordinary strenuousness, sincerity, and insight with which he first idealises and glorifies the vast universe around us, and then makes of it, not a theatre on which men play their parts, but an animate presence, intermingling with our works, pouring its companionable spirit about us, and "breathing grandeur upon the very humblest face of human life." This twofold and conjoint performance, consciously and expressly—perhaps only too consciously—undertaken by a man of strong inborn sensibility to natural impressions, and systematically carried out in a lifetime of brooding meditation and active composition, is Wordsworth's distinguishing title to fame and gratitude. In "words that speak of nothing more than what we are," he revealed new faces of nature; he dwelt on men as they are, men themselves; he strove to do that which has been declared to be the true secret of force in art, to make the trivial serve the expression of the sublime. "Wordsworth's distinctive work," Mr. Ruskin has justly said (*Modern Painters*, iii. 293), "was a war with pomp and pretence, and a display of the majesty of simple feelings and humble hearts, together with high reflective truth in his analysis of the courses of politics and ways of men; without these, his love of nature would have been comparatively worthless."

Yet let us not forget that he possessed the gift which to an artist is the very root of the matter. He saw Nature truly, he saw her as she is, and with his own eyes. The critic whom I have just quoted boldly pronounces him "the keenest eyed of all modern poets for what is deep and essential in nature." When he describes the daisy, casting the beauty of its star-shaped shadow on the smooth stone, or the boundless depth of the abysses of the sky, or the clouds made vivid as fire by the rays of light, every touch is true, not the copying of a literary phrase, but the result of direct observation.

It is true that Nature has sides to which Wordsworth was not energetically alive—Nature "red in tooth and claw." He was not energetically alive to the blind and remorseless cruelties of life and the world. When in early spring he heard the blended notes of the birds, and saw the budding twigs and primrose tufts, it grieved him, amid such fair works of nature, to think "what man has made of man." As if nature itself, excluding the conscious doings of that portion of nature which is the human race, and excluding also nature's own share in the making of poor Man, did not abound in raking cruelties and horrors of her own. "*Edel sei der Mensch,*" sang Goethe in a noble psalm, "*Hulfreich und gut, Denn das allein unterscheidet ihn, Von allen Wesen die wir kennen.*" "*Let man be noble, helpful, and good, for that alone distinguishes him from all beings that we know. No feeling has nature: to good and bad gives the sun his light, and for the evildoer as for the best shine moon and stars.*" That the laws which nature has fixed for our lives are mighty and eternal, Wordsworth comprehended as fully as Goethe, but not that they are laws pitiless as iron. Wordsworth had not rooted in him the sense of Fate—of the inexorable sequences of things, of the terrible chain that so often binds an awful end to some slight and trivial beginning.

This optimism or complacency in Wordsworth will be understood if we compare his spirit and treatment with that of the illustrious French painter whose subjects and whose life were in some ways akin to his own. Millet, like Wordsworth, went to the realities of humble life for his inspiration. The peasant of the great French plains and the forest was to him what the Cumbrian dalesman was to Wordsworth. But he saw the peasant differently. "You watch figures in the fields," said Millet, "digging and delving with spade or pick. You see one of them from time to time straightening his loins, and wiping his face with the back of his hand. Thou shalt eat thy bread in the sweat of thy brow. Is that the gay lively labour in which some people would have you believe? Yet it is there that for me you must seek true humanity and great poetry. They say that I deny the charm of the country; I find in it far more than charms, I find infinite splendours. I see in it, just as they do, the little flowers of which Christ said that Solomon in all his glory was not arrayed like one of them. I see clearly enough the sun as he spreads his splendour amid the clouds. None the less do I see on the plain, all smoking, the horses at the plough. I see in some stony corner a man all worn out, whose *han han* have been heard ever since daybreak—trying to straighten himself a moment to get breath." The hardness, the weariness, the sadness, the ugliness, out of which Millet's consummate skill made pictures that affect us like strange music, were to Wordsworth not the real part of the thing. They were all absorbed in the thought of nature as a whole, wonderful, mighty, harmonious, and benign.

We are not called upon to place great men of his stamp as if they were collegians in a class-list. It is best to take with thankfulness and admiration from each man what he has to give. What Wordsworth does is to assuage, to reconcile, to fortify. He has not Shakespeare's richness and vast compass, nor Milton's sublime and unflagging strength, nor Dante's severe, vivid, ardent force of vision. Probably he is too deficient in clear beauty of form and in concentrated power to be classed by the ages among these great giants. We cannot be sure. We may leave it to the ages to decide. But Wordsworth, at any rate, by his secret of bringing the infinite into common life, as he evokes it out of common life, has the skill to lead us, so long as we yield ourselves to his influence, into inner moods of settled peace, to touch "the depth and not the tumult of the soul," to give us quietness, strength, steadfastness, and purpose, whether to do or to endure. All art or poetry that has the effect of breathing into men's hearts, even if it be only for a space, these moods of settled peace, and strongly confirming their judgment and their will for good,— whatever limitations may be found besides, however prosaic may be some or much of the detail,—is great art and noble poetry, and the creator of it will always hold, as Wordsworth holds, a sovereign title to the reverence and gratitude of mankind.

A CHAPTER FROM
Studies in Literature, 1890

WORDSWORTH'S ETHICS.

By Leslie Stephen

Under every poetry, it has been said, there lies a philosophy. Rather, it may almost be said, every poetry is a philosophy. The poet and the philosopher live in the same world and are interested in the same truths. What is the nature of man and the world in which he lives, and what, in consequence, should be our conduct? These are the great problems, the answers to which may take a religious, a poetical, a philosophical, or an artistic form. The difference is that the poet has intuitions, while the philosopher gives demonstrations; that the thought which in one mind is converted into emotion, is in the other resolved into logic; and that a symbolic representation of the idea is substituted for a direct expression. The normal relation is exhibited in the case of the anatomist and the sculptor. The artist intuitively recognises the most perfect form; the man of science analyses the structural relations by which it is produced. Though the two provinces are concentric, they are not coincident. The reasoner is interested in many details which have no immediate significance for the man of feeling; and the poetic insight, on the other hand, is capable of recognising subtle harmonies and discords of which our crude instruments of weighing and measuring are incapable of revealing the secret. But the connection is so close that the greatest works of either kind seem to have a double nature. A philosophy may, like Spinoza's, be apparelled in the most technical and abstruse panoply of logic, and yet the total impression may stimulate a religious sentiment as effectively as any poetic or theosophic mysticism. Or a great imaginative work, like Shakespeare's, may

128

present us with the most vivid concrete symbols, and yet suggest, as forcibly as the formal demonstrations of a metaphysician, the idealist conviction that the visible and tangible world is a dream-woven tissue covering infinite and inscrutable mysteries. In each case the highest intellectual faculty manifests itself in the vigour with which certain profound conceptions of the world and life have been grasped and assimilated. In each case that man is greatest who soars habitually to the highest regions and gazes most steadily upon the widest horizons of time and space. The logical consistency which frames all dogmas into a consistent whole, is but another aspect of the imaginative power which harmonises the strongest and subtlest emotions excited.

The task, indeed, of deducing the philosophy from the poetry, of inferring what a man thinks from what he feels, may at times perplex the acutest critic. Nor, if it were satisfactorily accomplished, could we infer that the best philosopher is also the best poet. Absolute incapacity for poetical expression may be combined with the highest philosophic power. All that can safely be said is that a man's thoughts, whether embodied in symbols or worked out in syllogisms, are more valuable in proportion as they indicate greater philosophical insight; and therefore that, *ceteris paribus*, that man is the greater poet whose imagination is most transfused with reason; who has the deepest truths to proclaim as well as the strongest feelings to utter.

Some theorists implicitly deny this principle by holding substantially that the poet's function is simply the utterance of a particular mood, and that, if he utters it forcibly and delicately, we have no more to ask. Even so, we should not admit that the thoughts suggested to a wise man by a prospect of death and eternity are of just equal value, if equally well expressed, with the thoughts suggested to a fool by the contemplation of a good dinner. But, in practice, the utterance of emotions can hardly be dissociated from the assertion of principles. Psychologists have shown, ever since the days of Berkeley, that when a man describes (as he thinks) a mere sensation, and says, for example,

'I see a house,' he is really recording the result of a complex logical process. A great painter and the dullest observer may have the same impressions of coloured blotches upon their retina. The great man infers the true nature of the objects which produce his sensations, and can therefore represent the objects accurately. The other sees only with his eyes, and can therefore represent nothing. There is thus a logic implied even in the simplest observation, and one which can be tested by mathematical rules as distinctly as a proposition in geometry.

When we have to find a language for our emotions instead of our sensations, we generally express the result of an incomparably more complex set of intellectual operations. The poet, in uttering his joy or sadness, often implies, in the very form of his language, a whole philosophy of life or of the universe. The explanation is given at the end of Shakespeare's familiar passage about the poet's eye:—

> Such tricks hath strong imagination,
> That, if it would but apprehend some joy,
> It comprehends some bringer of that joy;
> Or in the night, imagining some fear,
> How easy is a bush supposed a bear!

The *ap*prehension of the passion, as Shakespeare logically says, is a *com*prehension of its cause. The imagination reasons. The bare faculty of sight involves thought and feeling. The symbol which the fancy spontaneously constructs, implies a whole world of truth or error, of superstitious beliefs or sound philosophy. The poetry holds a number of intellectual dogmas in solution; and it is precisely due to these general dogmas, which are true and important for us as well as for the poet, that his power over our sympathies is due. If his philosophy has no power in it, his emotions lose their hold upon our minds, or interest us only as antiquarians and lovers of the picturesque. But in the briefest poems of a true thinker we read the essence of the life-long reflections of a passionate and intellectual nature. Fears and hopes common to all thoughtful men have been coined into a single phrase. Even in cases where no definite conviction is expressed or even implied, and the poem is simply, like music, an indefinite utterance of a certain state of the emotions, we may discover an intellectual element. The rational and the emotional nature have such intricate relations that one cannot exist in great richness and force without justifying an inference as to the other. From a single phrase, as from a single gesture, we can often go far to divining the character of a man's thoughts and feelings. We know more of a man from five minutes' talk than from pages of what is called 'psychological analysis.' From a passing expression on the face, itself the result of variations so minute as to defy all analysis, we instinctively frame judgments as to a man's temperament and habitual modes of thought and conduct. Indeed, such judgments, if erroneous, determine us only too exclusively in the most important relations of life.

Now the highest poetry is that which expresses the richest, most powerful, and most susceptible emotional nature, and the most versatile, penetrative, and subtle intellect. Such qualities may be stamped upon trifling work. The great artist can express his power within the limits of a coin or a gem. The great poet will reveal his character through a sonnet or a song. Shakespeare, or Milton, or Burns, or Wordsworth can express his whole mode of feeling within a few lines. An ill-balanced nature reveals itself by a discord, as an illogical mind by a fallacy. A man need not compose an epic on a system of philosophy to write himself down an ass. And, inversely, a great mind and a noble nature may show itself by impalpable but recognisable signs within the 'sonnet's scanty plot of ground.' Once more, the highest poetry must be that which expresses not only the richest but the healthiest nature. Disease means an absence or a want of balance of certain faculties, and therefore leads to false reasoning or emotional discord. The defect of character betrays itself in some erroneous mode of thought or baseness of sentiment. And since morality means obedience to those rules which are most essential to the spiritual health, vicious feeling indicates some morbid tendency, and is so far destructive of the poetical faculty. An immoral sentiment is the sign either of a false judgment of the world and of human nature, or of a defect in the emotional nature which shows itself by a discord or an indecorum, and leads to a cynicism or indecency which offends the reason through the taste. What is called immorality does not indeed always imply such defects. Sound moral intuitions may be opposed to the narrow code prevalent at the time; or a protest against puritanical or ascetic perversions of the standard may hurry the poet into attacks upon true principles. And, again, the keen sensibility which makes a man a poet, undoubtedly exposes him to certain types of disease. He is more likely than his thick-skinned neighbour to be vexed by evil, and to be drawn into distorted views of life by an excess of sympathy or indignation. Injudicious admirers prize the disease instead of the strength from which it springs; and value the cynicism or the despair instead of the contempt for heartless commonplace or the desire for better things with which it was unfortunately connected. A strong moral sentiment has a great value, even when forced into an unnatural alliance. Nay, even when it is, so to speak, inverted, it often receives a kind of paradoxical value from its efficacy against some opposite form of error. It is only a complete absence of the moral faculty which is irredeemably bad. The poet in whom it does not exist is condemned to the lower sphere, and can only deal with the deepest feelings on penalty of shocking us by indecency or profanity. A man who can revel in 'Epicurus' stye' without even the indirect homage to purity of remorse and bitterness, can do nothing but gratify our lowest passions. They, perhaps, have their place, and the man who is content with such utterances may not be utterly worthless. But to place him on a level with his betters is to confound every sound principle of criticism.

It follows that a kind of collateral test of poetical excellence may be found by extracting the philosophy from the poetry.

The test is, of course, inadequate. A good philosopher may be an execrable poet. Even stupidity is happily not inconsistent with sound doctrine, though inconsistent with a firm grasp of ultimate principles. But the vigour with which a man grasps and assimilates a deep moral doctrine is a test of the degree in which he possesses one essential condition of the higher poetical excellence. A continuous illustration of this principle is given in the poetry of Wordsworth, who, indeed, has expounded his ethical and philosophical views so explicitly, one would rather not say so ostentatiously, that great part of the work is done to our hands. Nowhere is it easier to observe the mode in which poetry and philosophy spring from the same root and owe their excellence to the same intellectual powers. So much has been said by the ablest critics of the purely poetical side of Wordsworth's genius, that I may willingly renounce the difficult task of adding or repeating. I gladly take for granted—what is generally acknowledged—that Wordsworth in his best moods reaches a greater height than any other modern Englishman. The word 'inspiration' is less forced when applied to his loftiest poetry than when used of any of his contemporaries. With defects too obvious to be mentioned, he can yet pierce furthest behind the veil; and embody most efficiently the thoughts and emotions which come to us in our most solemn and reflective moods. Other poetry becomes trifling when we are making our inevitable passages through the Valley of the Shadow of Death. Wordsworth's alone retains its power. We love him the more as we grow older and become more deeply impressed with the sadness and seriousness of life; we are apt to grow weary of his rivals when we have finally quitted the regions of youthful enchantment. And I take the explanation to be that he is not merely a melodious writer, or a powerful utterer of deep emotion, but a true philosopher. His poetry wears well because it has solid substance. He is a prophet and a moralist, as well as a mere singer. His ethical system, in particular, is as distinctive and capable of systematic exposition as that of Butler. By endeavouring to state it in plain prose, we

133

shall see how the poetical power implies a sensitiveness to ideas which, when extracted from the symbolical embodiment, fall spontaneously into a scientific system of thought.

There are two opposite types to which all moral systems tend. They correspond to the two great intellectual families to which every man belongs by right of birth. One class of minds is distinguished by its firm grasp of facts, by its reluctance to drop solid substance for the loveliest shadows, and by its preference of concrete truths to the most symmetrical of theories. In ethical questions the tendency of such minds is to consider man as a being impelled by strong but unreasonable passions towards tangible objects. He is a loving, hating, thirsting, hungering—anything but a reasoning—being. As Swift—a typical example of this intellectual temperament—declared, man is not an *animal rationale*, but at most *capax rationis*. At bottom, he is a machine worked by blind instincts. Their tendency cannot be deduced by *à priori* reasoning, though reason may calculate the consequences of indulging them. The passions are equally good, so far as equally pleasurable. Virtue means that course of conduct which secures the maximum of pleasure. Fine theories about abstract rights and correspondence to eternal truths are so many words. They provide decent masks for our passions; they do not really govern them, or alter their nature, but they cover the ugly brutal selfishness of mankind, and soften the shock of conflicting interests. Such a view has something in it congenial to the English love of reality and contempt for shams. It may be represented by Swift or Mandeville in the last century; in poetry it corresponds to the theory attributed by some critics to Shakespeare; in a tranquil and reasoning mind it leads to the utilitarianism of Bentham; in a proud, passionate, and imaginative mind it manifests itself in such a poem as 'Don Juan.' Its strength is in its grasp of fact; its weakness, in its tendency to cynicism. Opposed to this is the school which starts from abstract reason. It prefers to dwell in the ideal world, where principles may be contemplated apart from the accidents which render them obscure to vulgar minds. It seeks to deduce the moral code from eternal truths without seeking for a groundwork in the facts of experience. If facts refuse to conform to theories, it proposes that facts should be summarily abolished. Though the actual human being is, unfortunately, not always reasonable, it holds that pure reason must be in the long run the dominant force, and that it reveals the laws to which mankind will ultimately conform. The revolutionary doctrine of the 'rights of man' expressed one form of this doctrine, and showed in the most striking way a strength and weakness, which are the converse of those exhibited by its antagonist. It was strong as appealing to the loftier motives of justice and sympathy; and weak as defying the appeal to experience. The most striking example in English literature is in Godwin's 'Political Justice.' The existing social order is to be calmly abolished because founded upon blind prejudice; the constituent atoms called men are to be rearranged in an ideal order as in a mathematical diagram. Shelley gives the translation of this theory into poetry. The 'Revolt of Islam' or the 'Prometheus Unbound,' with all its unearthly beauty, wearies the imagination which tries to soar into the thin air of Shelley's dreamworld; just as the intellect, trying to apply the abstract formulæ of political metaphysics to any concrete problem, feels as though it were under an exhausted receiver. In both cases we seem to have got entirely out of the region of real human passions and senses into a world, beautiful perhaps, but certainly impalpable.

The great aim of moral philosophy is to unite the disjoined element, to end the divorce between reason and experience, and to escape from the alternative of dealing with empty but symmetrical formulæ or concrete and chaotic facts. No hint can be given here as to the direction in which a final solution must be sought. Whatever the true method, Wordsworth's mode of conceiving the problem shows how powerfully he grasped the questions at issue. If his doctrines are not systematically expounded, they all have a direct bearing upon the real difficulties involved. They are stated so forcibly in his noblest poems that we might almost express a complete theory in his own language. But, without seeking to make a collection of aphorisms from his poetry, we may indicate the cardinal points of his teaching.[1]

The most characteristic of all his doctrines is that which is embodied in the great ode upon the 'Intimations of Immortality.' The doctrine itself—the theory that the instincts of childhood testify to the pre-existence of the soul—sounds fanciful enough; and Wordsworth took rather unnecessary pains to say that he did not hold it as a serious dogma. We certainly need not ask whether it is reasonable or orthodox to believe that 'our birth is but a sleep and a forgetting.' The fact symbolised by the poetic fancy— the glory and freshness of our childish instincts—is equally noteworthy, whatever its cause. Some modern reasoners would explain its significance by reference to a very different kind of pre-existence. The instincts, they would say, are valuable, because they register the accumulated and inherited experience of past generations. Wordsworth's delight in wild scenery is regarded by them as due to the 'combination of states that were organised in the race during barbarous times, when its pleasurable activities were amongst the mountains, woods, and waters.' In childhood we are most completely under the dominion of these inherited impulses. The correlation between the organism and its medium is then most perfect, and hence the peculiar theme of childish communion with nature.

Wordsworth would have repudiated the doctrine with disgust. He would have been 'on the side of the angels.' No memories of the savage and the monkey, but the reminiscences of the once-glorious soul could explain his emotions. Yet there is this much in common between him and the men of science whom he denounced with too little discrimination. The fact of the value of these primitive instincts is admitted, and admitted for the same purpose. Man, it is agreed, is furnished with sentiments which cannot be explained as the result of his individual experience. They may be intelligible, according to the evolutionist, when regarded as embodying the past experience of the race; or, according to

Wordsworth, as implying a certain mysterious faculty imprinted upon the soul. The scientific doctrine, whether sound or not, has modified the whole mode of approaching ethical problems; and Wordsworth, though with a very different purpose, gives a new emphasis to the facts, upon a recognition of which, according to some theorists, must be based the reconciliation of the great rival schools—the intuitionists and the utilitarians. The parallel may at first sight seem fanciful; and it would be too daring to claim for Wordsworth the discovery of the most remarkable phenomenon which modern psychology must take into account. There is, however, a real connection between the two doctrines, though in one sense they are almost antithetical. Meanwhile we observe that the same sensibility which gives poetical power is necessary to the scientific observer. The magic of the ode, and of many other passages in Wordsworth's poetry, is due to his recognition of this mysterious efficacy of our childish instincts. He gives emphasis to one of the most striking facts of our spiritual experience, which had passed with little notice from professed psychologists. He feels what they afterwards tried to explain.

The full meaning of the doctrine comes out as we study Wordsworth more thoroughly. Other poets—almost all poets— have dwelt fondly upon recollections of childhood. But not feeling so strongly, and therefore not expressing so forcibly, the peculiar character of the emotion, they have not derived the same lessons from their observation. The Epicurean poets are content with Herrick's simple moral—

Gather ye rosebuds while ye may—

and with his simple explanation—

That age is best which is the first,
When youth and blood are warmer.

Others more thoughtful look back upon the early days with the passionate regret of Byron's verses:

> There's not a joy the world can give like
>   that it takes away,
> When the glow of early thought declines
>   in feeling's dull decay;
> 'Tis not on youth's smooth cheek the
>   blush alone which fades so fast,
> But the tender bloom of heart is gone,
>   ere youth itself be past.

Such painful longings for the 'tender grace of a day that is dead' are spontaneous and natural. Every healthy mind feels the pang in proportion to the strength of its affections. But it is also true that the regret resembles too often the maudlin meditation of a fast young man over his morning's soda-water. It implies, that is, a non-recognition of the higher uses to which the fading memories may still be put. A different tone breathes in Shelley's pathetic but rather hectic moralisings, and his lamentations over the departure of the 'spirit of delight.' Nowhere has it found more exquisite expression than in the marvellous 'Ode to the West Wind.' These magical verses—his best, as it seems to me—describe the reflection of the poet's own mind in the strange stir and commotion of a dying winter's day. They represent, we may say, the fitful melancholy which oppresses a noble spirit when it has recognised the difficulty of forcing facts into conformity with the ideal. He still clings to the hope that his 'dead thoughts' may be driven over the universe,

> Like withered leaves to quicken a new birth.

But he bows before the inexorable fate which has cramped his energies:

A heavy weight of years has chained and bowed
One too like thee; tameless and swift and proud.

Neither Byron nor Shelley can see any satisfactory solution, and therefore neither can reach a perfect harmony of feeling. The world seems to them to be out of joint, because they have not known how to accept the inevitable, nor to conform to the discipline of facts. And, therefore, however intense the emotion, and however exquisite its expression, we are left in a state of intellectual and emotional discontent. Such utterances may suit us in youth, when we can afford to play with sorrow. As we grow older we feel a certain emptiness in them. A true man ought not to sit down and weep with an exhausted debauchee. He cannot afford to confess himself beaten with the idealist who has discovered that Rome was not built in a day, nor revolutions made with rose-water. He has to work as long as he has strength; to work in spite of, even by strength of, sorrow, disappointment, wounded vanity, and blunted sensibilities; and therefore he must search for some profounder solution for the dark riddle of life.

This solution it is Wordsworth's chief aim to supply. In the familiar verses which stand as a motto to his poems—

The child is father to the man,
And I could wish my days to be
Bound each to each by natural piety—

the great problem of life, that is, as he conceives it, is to secure a continuity between the period at which we are guided by half-conscious instincts, and that in which a man is able to supply the place of these primitive impulses by reasoned convictions. This is the thought which comes over and over again in his deepest poems, and round which all his teaching centred. It supplies the great moral, for example, of the 'Leech-gatherer:'

My whole life I have lived in pleasant thought,
As if life's business were a summer mood:
As if all needful things would come unsought
To genial faith still rich in genial good.

When his faith is tried by harsh experience, the leech-gatherer comes,

Like a man from some far region sent
To give me human strength by apt admonishment;

for he shows how the 'genial faith' may be converted into permanent strength by resolution and independence. The verses most commonly quoted, such as—

We poets in our youth begin in gladness,
But thereof come in the end despondency and sadness,

give the ordinary view of the sickly school. Wordsworth's aim is to supply an answer worthy not only of a poet, but a man. The same sentiment again is expressed in the grand 'Ode to Duty,' where the

Stern daughter of the voice of God

is invoked to supply that 'genial sense of youth' which has hitherto been a sufficient guidance; or in the majestic morality of the 'Happy Warrior;' or in the noble verses on 'Tintern Abbey;' or, finally, in the great ode which gives most completely the whole theory of that process by which our early intuitions are to be transformed into settled principles of feeling and action.

Wordsworth's philosophical theory, in short, depends upon the asserted identity between our childish instincts and our enlightened reason. The doctrine of a state of pre-existence, as it appears in other writers—as, for example, in the Cambridge

Platonists[2]—was connected with an obsolete metaphysical system, and the doctrine—exploded in its old form—of innate ideas. Wordsworth does not attribute any such preternatural character to the 'blank misgivings' and 'shadowy recollections' of which he speaks. They are invaluable data of our spiritual experience; but they do not entitle us to lay down dogmatic propositions independently of experience. They are spontaneous products of a nature in harmony with the universe in which it is placed, and inestimable as a clear indication that such a harmony exists. To interpret and regulate them belongs to the reasoning faculty and the higher imagination of later years. If he does not quite distinguish between the province of reason and emotion—the most difficult of philosophical problems—he keeps clear of the cruder mysticism, because he does not seek to elicit any definite formulæ from those admittedly vague forebodings which lie on the border-land between the two sides of our nature. With his invariable sanity of mind, he more than once notices the difficulty of distinguishing between that which nature teaches us and the interpretations which we impose upon nature.[3] He carefully refrains from pressing the inference too far.

The teaching, indeed, assumes that view of the universe which is implied in his pantheistic language. The Divinity really reveals Himself in the lonely mountains and the starry heavens. By contemplating them we are able to rise into that 'blessed mood' in which for a time the burden of the mystery is rolled off our souls, and we can 'see into the life of things.' And here we must admit that Wordsworth is not entirely free from the weakness which generally besets thinkers of this tendency. Like Shaftesbury in the previous century, who speaks of the universal harmony as emphatically though not as poetically as Wordsworth, he is tempted to adopt a too facile optimism. He seems at times to have overlooked that dark side of nature which is recognised in theological doctrines of corruption, or in the scientific theories about the fierce struggle for existence. Can we in fact say that these early instincts prove more than the happy constitution of the individual who feels them? Is there not a teaching of nature very apt to suggest horror and despair rather than a complacent brooding over soothing thoughts? Do not the mountains which Wordsworth loved so well, speak of decay and catastrophe in every line of their slopes? Do they not suggest the helplessness and narrow limitations of man, as forcibly as his possible exaltation? The awe which they strike into our souls has its terrible as well as its amiable side; and in moods of depression the darker aspect becomes more conspicuous than the brighter. Nay, if we admit that we have instincts which are the very substance of all that afterwards becomes ennobling, have we not also instincts which suggest a close alliance with the brutes? If the child amidst his newborn blisses suggests a heavenly origin, does he not also show sensual and cruel instincts which imply at least an admixture of baser elements? If man is responsive to all natural influences, how is he to distinguish between the good and the bad, and, in short, to frame a conscience out of the vague instincts which contain the germs of all the possible developments of the future?

To say that Wordsworth has not given a complete answer to such difficulties, is to say that he has not explained the origin of evil. It may be admitted, however, that he does to a certain extent show a narrowness of conception. The voice of nature, as he says, resembles an echo; but we 'unthinking creatures' listen to 'voices of two different natures.' We do not always distinguish between the echo of our lower passions and the 'echoes from beyond the grave.' Wordsworth sometimes fails to recognise the ambiguity of the oracle to which he appeals. The 'blessed mood' in which we get rid of the burden of the world, is too easily confused with the mood in which we simply refuse to attend to it. He finds lonely meditation so inspiring that he is too indifferent to the troubles of less self-sufficing or clear-sighted human beings. The ambiguity makes itself felt in the sphere of morality. The ethical doctrine that virtue consists in conformity to nature becomes ambiguous with him, as with all its advocates, when we ask for a precise definition of nature. How are we to know which natural forces make for us and which fight against us?

The doctrine of the love of nature, generally regarded as Wordsworth's great lesson to mankind, means, as interpreted by himself and others, a love of the wilder and grander objects of natural scenery; a passion for the 'sounding cataract,' the rock, the mountain, and the forest; a preference, therefore, of the country to the town, and of the simpler to the more complex forms of social life. But what is the true value of this sentiment? The unfortunate Solitary in the 'Excursion' is beset by three Wordsworths; for the Wanderer and the Pastor are little more (as Wordsworth indeed intimates) than reflections of himself, seen in different mirrors. The Solitary represents the anti-social lessons to be derived from communion with nature. He has become a misanthrope, and has learnt from 'Candide' the lesson that we clearly do not live in the best of all possible worlds. Instead of learning the true lesson from nature by penetrating its deeper meanings, he manages to feed

Pity and scorn and melancholy pride

by accidental and fanciful analogies, and sees in rock pyramids or obelisks a rude mockery of human toils. To confute this sentiment, to upset 'Candide,'

This dull product of a scoffer's pen,

is the purpose of the lofty poetry and versified prose of the long dialogues which ensue. That Wordsworth should call Voltaire dull is a curious example of the proverbial blindness of controversialists; but the moral may be equally good. It is given most pithily in the lines—

We live by admiration, hope, and love;
And even as these are well and wisely fused,
The dignity of being we ascend.

'But what is Error?' continues the preacher; and the Solitary replies by saying, 'somewhat haughtily,' that love, admiration, and hope are 'mad fancy's favourite vassals.' The distinction between fancy and imagination is, in brief, that fancy deals with the superficial resemblances, and imagination with the deeper truths which underlie them. The purpose, then, of the 'Excursion,' and of Wordsworth's poetry in general, is to show how the higher faculty reveals a harmony which we overlook when, with the Solitary, we

Skim along the surfaces of things.

The rightly prepared mind can recognise the divine harmony which underlies all apparent disorder. The universe is to its perceptions like the shell whose murmur in a child's ear seems to express a mysterious union with the sea. But the mind must be rightly prepared. Everything depends upon the point of view. One man, as he says in an elaborate figure, looking upon a series of ridges in spring from their northern side, sees a waste of snow, and from the south a continuous expanse of green. That view, we must take it, is the right one which is illuminated by the 'ray divine.' But we must train our eyes to recognise its splendour; and the final answer to the Solitary is therefore embodied in a series of narratives, showing by example how our spiritual vision may be purified or obscured. Our philosophy must be finally based, not upon abstract speculation and metaphysical arguments, but on the diffused consciousness of the healthy mind. As Butler sees the universe by the light of conscience, Wordsworth sees it through the wider emotions of awe, reverence, and love, produced in a sound nature.

The pantheistic conception, in short, leads to an unsatisfactory optimism in the general view of nature, and to an equal tolerance of all passions as equally 'natural.' To escape from this difficulty we must establish some more discriminative mode of interpreting nature. Man is the instrument played upon by all impulses, good or bad. The music which results may be harmonious or discordant. When the instrument is in tune, the music will be perfect; but when is it in tune, and how are we to know that it is in tune? That problem once solved, we can tell which are the authentic utterances and which are the accidental discords. And by solving it, or by saying what is the right constitution of human beings, we shall discover which is the true philosophy of the universe, and what are the dictates of a sound moral sense. Wordsworth implicitly answers the question by explaining, in his favourite phrase, how we are to build up our moral being.

The voice of nature speaks at first in vague emotions, scarcely distinguishable from mere animal buoyancy. The boy, hooting in mimicry of the owls, receives in his heart the voice of mountain torrents and the solemn imagery of rocks, and woods, and stars. The sportive girl is unconsciously moulded into stateliness and grace by the floating clouds, the bending willow, and even by silent sympathy with the motions of the storm. Nobody has ever shown, with such exquisite power as Wordsworth, how much of the charm of natural objects in later life is due to early associations, thus formed in a mind not yet capable of contemplating its own processes. As old Matthew says in the lines which, however familiar, can never be read without emotion—

My eyes are dim with childish tears,
    My heart is idly stirred;
For the same sound is in my ears
    Which in those days I heard.

And the strangely beautiful address to the cuckoo might be made into a text for a prolonged commentary by an æsthetic philosopher upon the power of early association. It curiously illustrates, for example, the reason of Wordsworth's delight in recalling sounds. The croak of the distant raven, the bleat of the mountain lamb, the splash of the leaping fish in the lonely tarn, are specially delightful to him, because the hearing is the most spiritual of our senses; and these sounds, like the cuckoo's cry, seem to convert the earth into an 'unsubstantial fairy place.' The phrase 'association' indeed implies a certain arbitrariness in the images suggested, which is not quite in accordance with Wordsworth's feeling. Though the echo depends partly upon the hearer, the mountain voices are specially adapted for certain moods. They have, we may say, a spontaneous affinity for the nobler affections. If some early passage in our childhood is associated with a particular spot, a house or a street will bring back the petty and accidental details: a mountain or a lake will revive the deeper and more permanent elements of feeling. If you have made love in a palace, according to Mr. Disraeli's prescription, the sight of it will recall the splendour of the object's dress or jewellery; if, as Wordsworth would prefer, with a background of mountains, it will appear in later days as if they had absorbed, and were always ready again to radiate forth, the tender and hallowing influences which then for the first time entered your life. The elementary and deepest passions are most easily associated with the sublime and beautiful in nature.

> The primal duties shine aloft like stars;
> The charities that soothe, and heal, and bless,
> Are scattered at the feet of man like flowers.

And, therefore, if you have been happy enough to take delight in these natural and universal objects in the early days, when the most permanent associations are formed, the sight of them in later days will bring back by pre-ordained and divine symbolism whatever was most ennobling in your early feelings. The vulgarising associations will drop off of themselves, and what was pure and lofty will remain.

From this natural law follows another of Wordsworth's favourite precepts. The mountains are not with him a symbol of anti-social feelings. On the contrary, they are in their proper place as the background of the simple domestic affections. He loves his native hills, not in the Byronic fashion, as a savage wilderness, but as the appropriate framework in which a healthy social order can permanently maintain itself. That, for example, is, as he tells us, the thought which inspired the 'Brothers,' a poem which excels all modern idylls in weight of meaning and depth of feeling, by virtue of the idea thus embodied. The retired valley of Ennerdale, with its grand background of hills, precipitous enough to be fairly called mountains, forces the two lads into closer affection. Shut in by these 'enormous barriers,' and undistracted by the ebb and flow of the outside world, the mutual love becomes concentrated. A tie like that of family blood is involuntarily imposed upon the little community of dalesmen. The image of sheep-tracks and shepherds clad in country grey is stamped upon the elder brother's mind, and comes back to him in tropical calms; he hears the tones of his waterfalls in the piping shrouds; and when he returns, recognises every fresh scar made by winter storms on the mountain sides, and knows by sight every unmarked grave in the little churchyard. The fraternal affection sanctifies the scenery, and the sight of the scenery brings back the affection with overpowering force upon his return. This is everywhere the sentiment inspired in Wordsworth by his beloved hills. It is not so much the love of nature pure and simple, as of nature seen through the deepest human feelings. The light glimmering in a lonely cottage, the one rude house in the deep valley, with its 'small lot of life-supporting fields and guardian rocks,' are necessary to point the moral and to draw to a definite focus the various forces of sentiment. The two veins of feeling are inseparably blended. The peasant noble, in the 'Song at the Feast of Brougham Castle,' learns equally from men and nature:—

147

Love had he found in huts where poor men lie;
　　His daily teachers had been woods and hills,
The silence that is in the starry skies,
　　The sleep that is among the lonely hills.

Without the love, the silence and the sleep would have had no spiritual meaning. They are valuable as giving intensity and solemnity to the positive emotion.

The same remark is to be made upon Wordsworth's favourite teaching of the advantages of the contemplative life. He is fond of enforcing the doctrine of the familiar lines, that we can feed our minds 'in a wise passiveness,' and that

One impulse from the vernal wood
　　Can teach you more of man,
Of moral evil and of good,
　　Than all the sages can.

And, according to some commentators, this would seem to express the doctrine that the ultimate end of life is the cultivation of tender emotions without reference to action. The doctrine, thus absolutely stated, would be immoral and illogical. To recommend contemplation in preference to action is like preferring sleeping to waking; or saying, as a full expression of the truth, that silence is golden and speech silvern. Like that familiar phrase, Wordsworth's teaching is not to be interpreted literally. The essence of such maxims is to be one-sided. They are paradoxical in order to be emphatic. To have seasons of contemplation, of withdrawal from the world and from books, of calm surrendering of ourselves to the influences of nature, is a practice commended in one form or other by all moral teachers. It is a sanitary rule, resting upon obvious principles. The mind which is always occupied in a multiplicity of small observations, or the regulation of practical details, loses the power of seeing general principles and of associating all objects with the central emotions of 'admiration, hope, and love.' The philosophic mind is that which habitually sees the general in the particular, and finds food for the deepest thought in the simplest objects. It requires, therefore, periods of repose, in which the fragmentary and complex atoms of distracted feeling which make up the incessant whirl of daily life may have time to crystallise round the central thoughts. But it must feed in order to assimilate; and each process implies the other as its correlative. A constant interest, therefore, in the joys and sorrows of our neighbours is as essential as quiet, self-centred rumination. It is when the eye 'has kept watch o'er man's mortality,' and by virtue of the tender sympathies of 'the human heart by which we live,' that to us

> The meanest flower which blows can give
> Thoughts that do often lie too deep for tears.

The solitude which implies severance from natural sympathies and affections is poisonous. The happiness of the heart which lives alone,

> Housed in a dream, an outcast from the kind,

* * * * *

> Is to be pitied, for 'tis surely blind.

Wordsworth's meditations upon flowers or animal life are impressive because they have been touched by this constant sympathy. The sermon is always in his mind, and therefore every stone may serve for a text. His contemplation enables him to see the pathetic side of the small pains and pleasures which we are generally in too great a hurry to notice. There are times, of course, when this moralising tendency leads him to the regions of the namby-pamby or sheer prosaic platitude. On the other hand, no one approaches him in the power of touching some rich chord of feeling by help of the pettiest incident. The old man going to the fox-hunt with a tear on his cheek, and saying to himself,

> The key I must take, for my Helen is dead;

or the mother carrying home her dead sailor's bird; the village schoolmaster, in whom a rift in the clouds revives the memory of his little daughter; the old huntsman unable to cut through the stump of rotten wood—touch our hearts at once and for ever. The secret is given in the rather prosaic apology for not relating a tale about poor Simon Lee:

> O reader! had you in your mind
>   Such stores as silent thought can bring,
> O gentle reader! you would find
>   A tale in everything.

The value of silent thought is so to cultivate the primitive emotions that they may flow spontaneously upon every common incident, and that every familiar object becomes symbolic of them. It is a familiar remark that a philosopher or man of science who has devoted himself to meditation upon some principle or law of nature, is always finding new illustrations in the most unexpected quarters. He cannot take up a novel or walk across the street without hitting upon appropriate instances. Wordsworth would apply the principle to the building up of our 'moral being.' Admiration, hope, and love should be so constantly in our thoughts, that innumerable sights and sounds which are meaningless to the world should become to us a language incessantly suggestive of the deepest topics of thought.

This explains his dislike to science, as he understood the word, and his denunciations of the 'world.' The man of science is one who cuts up nature into fragments, and not only neglects their possible significance for our higher feelings, but refrains on principle from taking it into account. The primrose suggests to him some new device in classification, and he would be worried by the suggestion of any spiritual significance as an annoying distraction. Viewing all objects 'in disconnection, dead and spiritless,' we are thus really waging

>An impious warfare with the very life
>Of our own souls.

We are putting the letter in place of the spirit, and dealing with nature as a mere grammarian deals with a poem. When we have learnt to associate every object with some lesson

>Of human suffering or of human joy;

when we have thus obtained the 'glorious habit,'

>By which sense is made
>Subservient still to moral purposes,
>Auxiliar to divine;

the 'dull eye' of science will light up; for, in observing natural processes, it will carry with it an incessant reference to the spiritual processes to which they are allied. Science, in short, requires to be brought into intimate connection with morality and religion. If we are forced for our immediate purpose to pursue truth for itself, regardless of consequences, we must remember all the more carefully that truth is a whole, and that fragmentary bits of knowledge become valuable as they are incorporated into a general system. The tendency of modern times to specialism brings with it a characteristic danger. It requires to be supplemented by a correlative process of integration. We must study details to increase our knowledge; we must accustom ourselves to look at the detail in the light of the general principles in order to make it fruitful.

The influence of that world which 'is too much with us late and soon' is of the same kind. The man of science loves barren facts for their own sake. The man of the world becomes devoted to some petty pursuit without reference to ultimate ends. He becomes a slave to money, or power, or praise, without caring for their effect upon his moral character. As social organisation becomes more complete, the social unit becomes a mere fragment instead of being a complete whole in himself. Man becomes

> The senseless member of a vast machine,
> Serving as doth a spindle or a wheel.

The division of labour, celebrated with such enthusiasm by Adam Smith,[4] tends to crush all real life out of its victims. The soul of the political economist may rejoice when he sees a human being devoting his whole faculties to the performance of one subsidiary operation in the manufacture of a pin. The poet and the moralist must notice with anxiety the contrast between the old-fashioned peasant who, if he discharged each particular function clumsily, discharged at least many functions, and found exercise for all the intellectual and moral faculties of his nature, and the modern artisan doomed to the incessant repetition of one petty set of muscular expansions and contractions, and whose soul, if he has one, is therefore rather an encumbrance than otherwise. This is the evil which is constantly before Wordsworth's eyes, as it has certainly not become less prominent since his time. The danger of crushing the individual is a serious one according to his view; not because it implies the neglect of some abstract political rights, but from the impoverishment of character which is implied in the process. Give every man a vote, and abolish all interference with each man's private tastes, and the danger may still be as great as ever. The tendency to 'differentiation'—as we call it in modern phraseology—the social pulverisation, the lowering and narrowing of the individual's sphere of action and feeling to the pettiest details, depends upon processes underlying all political changes. It cannot, therefore, be cured by any nostrum of constitution-mongers, or by the negative remedy of removing old barriers. It requires to be met by profounder moral and religious teaching. Men must be taught what is the really valuable part of their natures, and what is the purest happiness to be extracted from life, as well as allowed to gratify fully their own tastes; for who can say that men encouraged by all their surroundings and appeals to the most obvious motives to turn themselves into machines, will not deliberately choose to be machines? Many powerful thinkers have illustrated Wordsworth's doctrine more elaborately, but nobody has gone more decisively to the root of the matter.

One other side of Wordsworth's teaching is still more significant and original. Our vague instincts are consolidated into reason by meditation, sympathy with our fellows, communion with nature, and a constant devotion to 'high endeavours.' If life run smoothly, the transformation may be easy, and our primitive optimism turn imperceptibly into general complacency. The trial comes when we make personal acquaintance with sorrow, and our early buoyancy begins to fail. We are tempted to become querulous or to lap ourselves in indifference. Most poets are content to bewail our lot melodiously, and admit that there is no remedy unless a remedy be found in 'the luxury of grief.' Prosaic people become selfish, though not sentimental. They laugh at their old illusions, and turn to the solid consolations of comfort. Nothing is more melancholy than to study many biographies, and note—not the failure of early promise, which may mean merely an aiming above the mark—but the progressive deterioration of character which so often follows grief and disappointment. If it be not true that most men grow worse as they grow old, it is surely true that few men pass through the world without being corrupted as much as purified.

Now Wordsworth's favourite lesson is the possibility of turning grief and disappointment into account.

He teaches in many forms the necessity of 'transmuting' sorrow into strength. One of the great evils is a lack of power,

> An agonising sorrow to transmute.

The Happy Warrior is, above all, the man who in face of all human miseries can

> Exercise a power
> Which is our human nature's highest dower;
> Controls them, and subdues, transmutes, bereaves
> Of their bad influence, and their good receives;

who is made more compassionate by familiarity with sorrow, more placable by contest, purer by temptation, and more enduring by distress.[5] It is owing to the constant presence of this thought, to his sensibility to the refining influence of sorrow, that Wordsworth is the only poet who will bear reading in times of distress. Other poets mock us by an impossible optimism, or merely reflect the feelings which, however we may play with them in times of cheerfulness, have now become an intolerable burden. Wordsworth suggests the single topic which, so far at least as this world is concerned, can really be called consolatory. None of the ordinary commonplaces will serve, or serve at most as indications of human sympathy. But there is some consolation in the thought that even death may bind the survivors closer, and leave as a legacy enduring motives to noble action. It is easy to say this; but Wordsworth has the merit of feeling the truth in all its force, and expressing it by the most forcible images. In one shape or another the sentiment is embodied in most of his really powerful poetry. It is intended, for example, to be the moral of the 'White Doe of Rylstone.' There, as Wordsworth says, everything fails so far as its object is external and unsubstantial; everything succeeds so far as it is moral and spiritual. Success grows out of failure; and the mode in which it grows is indicated by the lines which give the keynote of the poem. Emily, the heroine, is to become a soul

> By force of sorrows high
> Uplifted to the purest sky
> Of undisturbed serenity.

The 'White Doe' is one of those poems which make many readers inclined to feel a certain tenderness for Jeffrey's dogged insensibility; and I confess that I am not one of its warm admirers. The sentiment seems to be unduly relaxed throughout; there is a want of sympathy with heroism of the rough and active type, which is, after all, at least as worthy of admiration as the more passive variety of the virtue; and the defect is made more palpable by the position of the chief actors. These rough borderers, who recall William of Deloraine and Dandie Dinmont, are somehow out of their element when preaching the doctrines of quietism and submission to circumstances. But, whatever our judgment of this particular embodiment of Wordsworth's moral philosophy, the inculcation of the same lesson gives force to many of his finest poems. It is enough to mention the 'Leech-gatherer,' the 'Stanzas on Peele Castle,' 'Michael,' and, as expressing the inverse view of the futility of idle grief, 'Laodamia,' where he has succeeded in combining his morality with more than his ordinary beauty of poetical form. The teaching of all these poems falls in with the doctrine already set forth. All moral teaching, I have sometimes fancied, might be summed up in the one formula, 'Waste not.' Every element of which our nature is composed may be said to be good in its proper place; and therefore every vicious habit springs out of the misapplication of forces which might be turned to account by judicious training. The waste of sorrow is one of the most lamentable forms of waste. Sorrow too often tends to produce bitterness or effeminacy of character. But it may, if rightly used, serve only to detach us from the lower motives, and give sanctity to the higher. That is what Wordsworth sees with unequalled clearness, and he therefore sees also the condition of profiting. The mind in which the most valuable elements have been systematically strengthened by meditation, by association of deep thought with the most universal presences, by constant sympathy with the joys and sorrows of its fellows, will be prepared to convert sorrow into a medicine instead of a poison. Sorrow is deteriorating so far as it is selfish.

The man who is occupied with his own interests makes grief an excuse for effeminate indulgence in self-pity. He becomes weaker and more fretful. The man who has learnt habitually to think of himself as part of a greater whole, whose conduct has been habitually directed to noble ends, is purified and strengthened by the spiritual convulsion. His disappointment, or his loss of some beloved object, makes him more anxious to fix the bases of his happiness widely and deeply, and to be content with the consciousness of honest work, instead of looking for what is called success.

But I must not take to preaching in the place of Wordsworth. The whole theory is most nobly summed up in the grand lines already noticed on the character of the Happy Warrior. There Wordsworth has explained in the most forcible and direct language the mode in which a grand character can be formed; how youthful impulses may change into manly purpose; how pain and sorrow may be transmuted into new forces; how the mind may be fixed upon lofty purposes; how the domestic affections—which give the truest happiness—may also be the greatest source of strength to the man who is

More brave for this, that he has much to lose;

and how, finally, he becomes indifferent to all petty ambition—

Finds comfort in himself and in his cause;
And, while the mortal mist is gathering, draws
His breath in confidence of Heaven's applause.

This is the Happy Warrior, this is he
Whom every man in arms should wish to be.

We may now see what ethical theory underlies Wordsworth's teaching of the transformation of instinct into reason. We must start from the postulate that there is in fact a Divine order in the universe; and that conformity to this order produces beauty as embodied in the external world, and is the condition of virtue as regulating our character. It is by obedience to the 'stern lawgiver,' Duty, that flowers gain their fragrance, and that 'the most ancient heavens' preserve their freshness and strength. But this postulate does not seek for justification in abstract metaphysical reasoning. The 'Intimations of Immortality' are precisely imitations, not intellectual intuitions. They are vague and emotional, not distinct and logical. They are a feeling of harmony, not a perception of innate ideas. And, on the other hand, our instincts are not a mere chaotic mass of passions, to be gratified without considering their place and function in a certain definite scheme. They have been implanted by the Divine hand, and the harmony which we feel corresponds to a real order. To justify them we must appeal to experience, but to experience interrogated by a certain definite procedure. Acting upon the assumption that the Divine order exists, we shall come to recognise it, though we could not deduce it by an *à priori* method.

The instrument, in fact, finds itself originally tuned by its Maker, and may preserve its original condition by careful obedience to the stern teaching of life. The buoyancy common to all youthful and healthy natures then changes into a deeper and more solemn mood. The great primary emotions retain the original impulse, but increase their volume. Grief and disappointment are transmuted into tenderness, sympathy, and endurance. The reason, as it develops, regulates, without weakening, the primitive instincts. All the greatest, and therefore most common, sights of nature are indelibly associated with 'admiration, hope, and love;' and all increase of knowledge and power is regarded as a means for furthering the gratification of our nobler emotions. Under the opposite treatment, the character loses its freshness, and we regard the early happiness as an illusion. The old emotions dry up at their source. Grief produces fretfulness, misanthropy, or effeminacy. Power is wasted on petty ends and frivolous excitement, and knowledge becomes barren and pedantic. In this way the postulate justifies itself by producing the noblest type of character. When the 'moral being' is thus built up, its instincts become its convictions, we recognise the true voice of nature, and distinguish it from the echo of our passions. Thus we come to know how the Divine order and the laws by which the character is harmonised are the laws of morality.

To possible objections it might be answered by Wordsworth that this mode of assuming in order to prove is the normal method of philosophy. 'You must love him,' as he says of the poet,

Ere to you
He will seem worthy of your love.

The doctrine corresponds to the *crede ut intelligas* of the divine; or to the philosophic theory that we must start from the knowledge already constructed within us by instincts which have not yet learnt to reason. And, finally, if a persistent reasoner should ask why—even admitting the facts—the higher type should be preferred to the lower, Wordsworth may ask, Why is bodily health preferable to disease? If a man likes weak lungs and a bad digestion, reason cannot convince him of his error. The physician has done enough when he has pointed out the sanitary laws obedience to which generates strength, long life, and power of enjoyment. The moralist is in the same position when he has shown how certain habits conduce to the development of a type superior to its rivals in all the faculties which imply permanent peace of mind and power of resisting the shocks of the world without disintegration. Much undoubtedly remains to be said. Wordsworth's teaching, profound and admirable as it may be, has not the potency to silence the scepticism which has gathered strength since his day, and assailed fundamental—or what to him seemed fundamental—tenets of his system. No one can yet say what transformation may pass upon the thoughts and emotions for which he found utterance in speaking of the Divinity and sanctity of nature. Some people vehemently maintain that the words will be emptied of all meaning if the old theological conceptions to which he was so firmly attached should disappear with the development of new modes of thought. Nature, as regarded by the light of modern science, will be the name of a cruel and wasteful, or at least of a purely neutral and indifferent power, or perhaps as merely an equivalent for the Unknowable, to which the conditions of our intellect prevent us from ever attaching any intelligible predicate. Others would say that in whatever terms we choose to speak of the mysterious darkness which surrounds our little island of comparative light, the emotion generated in a thoughtful mind by the contemplation of the universe will remain unaltered or strengthen with clearer knowledge; and that we shall express ourselves in a new dialect without altering the essence of our thought. The emotions to which Wordsworth has given utterance will remain, though the system in which he believed should sink into oblivion; as, indeed, all human systems have found different modes of symbolising the same fundamental feelings. But it is enough vaguely to indicate considerations not here to be developed.

It only remains to be added once more that Wordsworth's poetry derives its power from the same source as his philosophy. It speaks to our strongest feelings because his speculation rests upon our deepest thoughts. His singular capacity for investing all objects with a glow derived from early associations; his keen sympathy with natural and simple emotions; his sense of the sanctifying influences which can be extracted from sorrow, are of equal value to his power over our intellects and our imaginations. His psychology, stated systematically, is rational; and, when expressed passionately, turns into poetry. To be sensitive to the most important phenomena is the first step equally towards a poetical or a scientific exposition. To see these truly is the condition of making the poetry harmonious and the philosophy logical. And it is often difficult to say which power is most remarkable in Wordsworth. It would be easy to illustrate the truth by other than moral topics. His sonnet, noticed by De Quincey, in which he speaks of the abstracting power of darkness, and observes that as the hills pass into twilight we see the same sight as the ancient Britons, is impressive as it stands, but would be equally good as an illustration in a metaphysical treatise. Again, the sonnet beginning

With ships the sea was sprinkled far and wide,

is at once, as he has shown in a commentary of his own, an illustration of a curious psychological law—of our tendency, that is, to introduce an arbitrary principle of order into a random collection of objects—and, for the same reason, a striking embodiment of the corresponding mood of feeling. The little poem called 'Stepping Westward' is in the same way at once a delicate expression of a specific sentiment and an acute critical analysis of the subtle associations suggested by a single phrase. But such illustrations might be multiplied indefinitely. As he has himself said, there is scarcely one of his poems which does not call attention to some moral sentiment, or to a general principle or law of thought, of our intellectual constitution.

Finally, we might look at the reverse side of the picture, and endeavour to show how the narrow limits of Wordsworth's power are connected with certain moral defects; with the want of quick sympathy which shows itself in his dramatic feebleness, and the austerity of character which caused him to lose his special gifts too early and become a rather commonplace defender of conservatism; and that curious diffidence (he assures us that it was 'diffidence') which induced him to write many thousand lines of blank verse entirely about himself. But the task would be superfluous as well as ungrateful. It was his aim, he tells us, 'to console the afflicted; to add sunshine to daylight by making the happy happier; to teach the young and the gracious of every age to see, to think, and therefore to become more actively and securely virtuous;' and, high as was the aim he did much towards its accomplishment.

FOOTNOTES:

[1] J. S. Mill and Whewell were, for their generation, the ablest exponents of two opposite systems of thought upon such matters. Mill has expressed his obligations to Wordsworth in his 'Autobiography,' and Whewell dedicated to Wordsworth his 'Elements of Morality' in acknowledgment of his influence as a moralist.

[2] The poem of Henry Vaughan, to which reference is often made in this connection, scarcely contains more than a pregnant hint.

[3] As, for example, in the *Lines on Tintern Abbey*: 'If this be but a vain belief.'

[4] See Wordsworth's reference to the *Wealth of Nations*, in the *Prelude*, book xiii.

[5] So, too, in the *Prelude*:—

> *Then was the truth received into my heart,*
> *That, under heaviest sorrow earth can bring,*
> *If from the affliction somewhere do not grow*
> *Honour which could not else have been, a faith,*
> *An elevation, and a sanctity;*
> *If new strength be not given, nor old restored,*
> *The fault is ours, not Nature's.*

TO WILLIAM WORDSWORTH.

THANKS FOR ADVICE.

A Letter By Charlotte Brontë

1840.

... Authors are generally very tenacious of their productions, but I am not so much attached to this but that I can give it up without much distress. No doubt, if I had gone on, I should have made quite a Richardsonian concern of it.... I had materials in my head for half-a-dozen volumes.... Of course, it is with considerable regret I relinquish any scheme so charming as the one I have sketched. It is very edifying and profitable to create a world out of your own brains, and people it with inhabitants, who are so many Melchisedecs, and have no father nor mother but your own imagination.... I am sorry I did not exist fifty or sixty years ago, when the Ladies' Magazine was flourishing like a green bay tree. In that case, I make no doubt, my aspirations after literary fame would have met with due encouragement, and I should have had the pleasure of introducing Messrs. Percy and West into the very best society, and recording all their sayings and doings in double-columned close-printed pages.... I recollect, when I was a child, getting hold of some antiquated volumes, and reading them by stealth with the most exquisite pleasure. You give a correct description of the patient Grisels of those days. My aunt was one of them; and to this day she thinks the tales of the Ladies' Magazine infinitely superior to any trash of modern literature. So do I; for I read them in childhood, and childhood has a very strong faculty of admiration, but a very weak one of criticism.... I am pleased that you cannot quite decide whether I am an attorney's clerk or a novel-reading dressmaker. I will not help you at all in the discovery; and as to my handwriting, or the ladylike touches in my style and imagery, you must not draw any conclusion from that—I may employ an amanuensis. Seriously, sir, I am very much obliged to you for your kind and candid letter. I almost wonder you took the trouble to read and notice the novelette of an anonymous scribe, who had not even the manners to tell you whether he was a man or a woman, or whether his 'C.T.' meant Charles Timms or Charlotte Tomkins.

AN EXCERPT FROM
Selected English Letters,
XV — XIX Centuries, 1913
ARRANGED BY
M. DUCKITT & H. WRAGG

TO WILLIAM WORDSWORTH.

THE DELIGHTS OF LONDON.

A Letter By Charles Lamb

30 Jan. 1801.

I ought before this to have replied to your very kind invitation into Cumberland. With you and your sister I could gang anywhere; but I am afraid whether I shall ever be able to afford so desperate a journey. Separate from the pleasure of your company, I don't much care if I never see a mountain in my life. I have passed all my days in London, until I have formed as many and intense local attachments as any of you mountaineers can have done with dead Nature. The lighted shops of the Strand and Fleet Street; the innumerable trades, tradesmen, and customers, coaches, waggons, playhouses; all the bustle and wickedness round about Covent Garden; the very women of the Town; the watchmen, drunken scenes, rattles;—life awake, if you awake, at all hours of the night; the crowds, the very dirt and mud, the sun shining upon houses and pavements, the printshops, the old book-stalls, parsons cheapening books, coffee-houses, steams of soups from kitchens, the pantomimes—London itself a pantomime and a masquerade—all these things work themselves into my mind, and feed me, without a power of satiating me. The wonder of these sights impels me often into night-walks about her crowded streets, and I often shed tears in the motley Strand from fullness of joy at so much life. All these emotions must be

164

strange to you; so are your rural emotions to me. But consider, what must I have been doing all my life, not to have lent great portions of my heart with usury to such scenes?

My attachments are all local, purely local. I have no passion (or have had none since I was in love, and then it was the spurious engendering of poetry and books) to groves and valleys. The rooms where I was born, the furniture which has been before my eyes all my life, a book-case which has followed me about like a faithful dog, (only exceeding him in knowledge,) wherever I have moved, old chairs, old tables, streets, squares, where I have sunned myself, my old school,—these are my mistresses,—have I not enough, without your mountains? I do not envy you. I should pity you, did I not know that the mind will make friends of anything. Your sun, and moon, and skies, and hills, and lakes, affect me no more, or scarcely come to me in more venerable characters, than as a gilded room with tapestry and tapers, where I might live with handsome visible objects. I consider the clouds above me but as a roof beautifully painted, but unable to satisfy the mind: and at last, like the pictures of the apartment of a connoisseur, unable to afford him any longer a pleasure. So fading upon me, from disuse, have been the beauties of Nature, as they have been confinedly called; so ever fresh, and green, and warm are all the inventions of men, and assemblies of men in this great city. I should certainly have laughed with dear Joanna.

Give my kindest love, and my sister's, to D. and yourself; and a kiss from me to little Barbara Lewthwaite.

Thank you for liking my play!

AN EXCERPT FROM
Selected English Letters,
XV — XIX Centuries, 1913
ARRANGED BY
M. DUCKITT & H. WRAGG

APPRECIATIONS.

By Pelham Edgar

Coleridge, with rare insight, summarized Wordsworth's characteristic defects and merits as follows;

"The first characteristic, though only occasional defect, which I appear to myself to find in these poems is the inconstancy of the style. Under this name I refer to the sudden and unprepared transitions from lines or sentences of peculiar felicity (at all events striking and original) to a style, not only unimpassioned but undistinguished.

"The second defect I can generalize with tolerable accuracy, if the reader will pardon an uncouth and newly-coined word. There is, I should say, not seldom a *matter-of-factness* in certain poems. This may be divided into, first, a laborious minuteness and fidelity in the representation of objects, and there positions, as they appeared to the poet himself; secondly, the insertion of accidental circumstances, in order to the full explanation of his living characters, their dispositions and actions; which circumstances might be necessary to establish the probability of a statement in real life, when nothing is taken for granted by the hearer; but appear superfluous in poetry, where the reader is willing to believe for his own sake. . .

"Third; an undue predilection for the *dramatic* form in certain poems, from which one or other of two evils result. Either the thoughts and diction are different from that of the poet, and then there arises an incongruity of style; or they are the same and indistinguishable, where two are represented as talking, while in truth one man only speaks. . .

"The fourth class of defects is closely connected with the former; but yet are such as arise likewise from an intensity of feeling disproportionate to such knowledge and value of the objects described, as can be fairly anticipated of men in general, even of the most cultivated classes; and with which therefore few only, and those few particularly circumstanced, can be supposed to sympathize: in this class, I comprise occasional prolixity, repetition, and an eddying, instead of progression, of thought. . .

"Fifth and last; thoughts and images too great for the subject. This is an approximation to what might be called mental bombast, as distinguished from verbal: for, as in the latter there is a disproportion of the expressions to the thoughts, so in this there is a disproportion of thought to the circumstance and occasion. . .

"To these defects, which . . . are only occasional, I may oppose the following (for the most part correspondent) excellencies:

"First; an austere purity of language both grammatically and logically; in short a perfect appropriateness of the words to the meaning. . .

"The second characteristic excellence of Mr. Wordsworth's works is—a correspondent weight and sanity of the thoughts and sentiments, won not from books, but from the poet's own meditative observations. They are fresh and have the dew upon them. . .

"Third; . . . the sinewy strength and originality of single lines and paragraphs; the frequent *curiosa felicitas* of his diction. . .

"Fourth; the perfect truth of nature in his images and descriptions as taken immediately from nature, and proving a long and genial intimacy with the very spirit which gives the physiognomic expressions to all the works of nature. Like a green field reflected in a calm and perfectly transparent lake, the image is distinguished from the reality only by its greater softness and lustre. Like the moisture or the polish on a pebble, genius neither distorts nor false-colors its objects; but on the contrary, brings out many a vein and many a tint, which escape the eye of common observation, thus raising to the rank of gems what had been often kicked away by the hurrying foot of the traveller on the dusty high-road of custom...

"Fifth; a meditative pathos, a union of deep and subtle thought with sensibility; a sympathy with man as man; the sympathy indeed of a contemplator, rather than a fellow-sufferer or co-mate, but of a contemplator, from whose view no difference of rank conceals the sameness of the nature; no injuries of wind or weather, of toil, or even of ignorance, wholly disguise the human face divine. The superscription and the image of the Creator still remains legible to *him* under the dark lines, with which guilt or calamity had cancelled or cross-barred it. Here the Man and the Poet lose and find themselves in each other, the one as glorified, the latter as substantiated. In this mild and philosophic pathos, Wordsworth appears to me without a compeer. Such as he is; so he writes.

"Last and pre-eminently, I challenge for this poet the gift of imagination in the highest and strictest sense of the word. In the play of fancy, Wordsworth, to my feelings, is not always graceful, and sometimes recondite... But in imaginative power, he stands nearest of all writers to Shakespeare and Milton; and yet in a kind perfectly unborrowed and his own."

These are the grounds upon which Coleridge bases the poetic claims of Wordsworth.

Matthew Arnold, in the preface to his well-known collection of Wordsworth's poems, accords to the poet a rank no less exalted. "I firmly believe that the poetical performance of Wordsworth is, after that of Shakespeare and Milton, of which all the world now recognizes the worth, undoubtedly the most considerable in our language from the Elizabethan age to the present time." His essential greatness is to be found in his shorter pieces, despite the frequent intrusion of much that is very inferior. Still it is "by the great body of powerful and significant work which remains to him after every reduction and deduction has been made, that Wordsworth's superiority is proved."

Coleridge had not dwelt sufficiently, perhaps, upon the joyousness which results from Wordsworth's philosophy of human life and external nature. This Matthew Arnold considers to be the prime source of his greatness. "Wordsworth's poetry is great because of the extraordinary power with which Wordsworth feels the joy offered to us in the simple primary affections and duties; and because of the extraordinary power with which, in case after case, he shows us this joy, and renders it so as to make us share it." Goethe's poetry, as Wordsworth once said, is not inevitable enough, is too consciously moulded by the supreme will of the artist. "But Wordsworth's poetry," writes Arnold, "when he is at his best, is inevitable, as inevitable as Nature herself. It might seem that Nature not only gave him the matter for his poem, but wrote his poem for him." The set poetic style of *The Excursion* is a failure, but there is something unique and unmatchable in the simple grace of his narrative poems and lyrics. "Nature herself seems, I say, to take the pen out of his hand, and to write for him with her own bare, sheer, penetrating power. This arises from two causes: from the profound sincereness with which Wordsworth feels his subject, and also from the profoundly sincere and natural character of his subject itself. He can and will treat such a subject with nothing but the most plain, first hand, almost austere naturalness. His expression may often be called bald, as, for instance, in the poem of *Resolution and Independence*; but it is bald as the bare mountain tops are bald, with a baldness which is full of grandeur. . . Wherever we meet with the successful balance, in Wordsworth, of profound truth of subject with profound truth of execution, he is unique."

Professor Dowden has also laid stress upon the harmonious balance of Wordsworth's nature, his different faculties seeming to interpenetrate one another, and yield mutual support. He has likewise called attention to the austere naturalism of which Arnold speaks. "Wordsworth was a great naturalist in literature, but he was also a great Idealist; and between the naturalist and the idealist in Wordsworth no opposition existed: each worked with the other, each served the other. While Scott, by allying romance with reality, saved romantic fiction from the extravagances and follies into which it had fallen, Wordsworth's special work was to open a higher way for naturalism in art by its union with ideal truth."

Criticism has long since ceased to ridicule his *Betty Foy*, and his *Harry Gill*, whose "teeth, they chatter, chatter still." Such malicious sport proved only too easy for Wordsworth's contemporaries, and still the essential value of his poetry was unimpaired.

The range of poetry is indeed inexhaustible, and even the greatest poets must suffer some subtraction from universal pre-eminence. Therefore we may frankly admit the deficiencies of Wordsworth,—that he was lacking in dramatic force and in the power of characterization; that he was singularly deficient in humor, and therefore in the saving grace of self-criticism in the capacity to see himself occasionally in a ridiculous light; that he has little of the romantic glamor and none of the narrative energy of Scott; that Shelley's lyrical flights leave him plodding along the dusty highway; and that Byron's preternatural force makes his passion seen by contrast pale and ineffectual. All this and more may freely be granted, and yet for his influence upon English thought, and especially upon the poetic thought of his country, he must be named after Shakespeare and Milton. The intellectual value of his work will endure; for leaving aside much valuable doctrine, which from didactic excess fails as poetry, he has brought into the world a new philosophy of Nature and has emphasised in a manner distinctively his own the dignity of simple manhood.—*Pelham Edgar.*

A CHAPTER FROM
Selections from Wordsworth and Tennyson, 1917

THE LAND
OF WORDSWORTH.

By William Winter

A good way by which to enter the Lake District of England is to travel to Penrith and thence to drive along the shore of Ullswater, or sail upon its crystal bosom, to the blooming solitude of Patterdale. Penrith lies at the eastern slope of the mountains of Westmoreland, and you may see the ruins of Penrith Castle, once the property and the abode of Richard, Duke of Gloucester, before he became King of England. Penrith Castle was one of the estates that were forfeited by the great Earl of Warwick, and King Edward the Fourth gave it to his brother Richard, in 1471. It is recorded that Richard had lived there for five years, from 1452 to 1457, when he was Sheriff of Cumberland. Not much remains of that ancient structure, and the remnant is now occupied by a florist. I saw it, as I saw almost everything else in Great Britain during the summer of 1888, under a tempest of rain; for it rained there, with a continuity almost ruinous, from the time of the lilac and apple-blossom till when the clematis began to show the splendour of its purple shield and the acacia to drop its milky blossoms on the autumnal grass. But travellers must not heed the weather. If there are dark days there are also bright ones,—and one bright day in such a paradise as the English Lakes atones for the dreariness of a month of rain. Besides, even the darkest days may be brightened by gentle companionship. Henry Irving and Ernest Bendall, two of the most intellectual and genial men in England, were my associates, in that expedition. We went from

171

London into Westmoreland on a mild, sweet day in July, and we rambled for several days in that enchanted region. It was a delicious experience, and I often close my eyes and dream of it—as I am dreaming now.

In the drive between Penrith and Patterdale you see many things that are worthy of regard. Among these are the parish church of Penrith, a building made of red stone, remarkable for a massive square tower of great age and formidable aspect. In the adjacent churchyard are The Giant's Grave and The Giant's Thumb, relics of a distant past that strongly and strangely affect the imagination. The grave is said to be that of Ewain Cæsarius, a gigantic individual who reigned over Cumberland in remote Saxon times. The Thumb is a rough stone, about seven feet high, presenting a clumsy cross, and doubtless commemorative of another mighty warrior. Sir Walter Scott, who traversed Penrith on his journeys between Edinburgh and London, seldom omitted to pause for a view of those singular memorials, and Scott, like Wordsworth, has left upon this region the abiding impress of his splendid genius. Ulfo's Lake is Scott's name for Ullswater, and thereabout is laid the scene of his poem of The Bridal of Triermain. In Scott's day the traveller went by coach or on horseback, but now, "By lonely Threlkeld's waste and wood," at the foot of craggy Blencathara, you pause at a railway station having Threlkeld in large letters on its official signboard. Another strange thing that is passed on the road between Penrith and Patterdale is "Arthur's Round Table,"—a circular terrace of turf slightly raised above the surrounding level, and certainly remarkable, whatever may be its historic or antiquarian merit, for fine texture, symmetrical form, and lovely, luxuriant colour. Scholars think it was used for tournaments in the days of chivalry, but no one rightly knows anything about it, save that it is old. Not far from this bit of mysterious antiquity the road winds through a quaint village called Tirril, where, in the Quaker burial-ground, is the grave of an unfortunate young man, Charles Gough, who lost his life by falling from the Striding Edge of Helvellyn in 1805,

172

and whose memory is hallowed by Wordsworth and Scott, in poems that almost every schoolboy has read, and could never forget,—associated as they are with the story of the faithful dog, for three months in that lonesome wilderness vigilant beside the dead body of his master,

> "A lofty precipice in front,
> A silent tarn below."

Patterdale possesses this advantage over certain other towns and hamlets of the lake region, that it is not much frequented by tourists. The coach does indeed roll through it at intervals, laden with those miscellaneous, desultory visitors whose pleasure it is to rush wildly over the land. And those objects serve to remind you that now, even as in Wordsworth's time, and in a double sense, "the world is too much with us." But an old-fashioned inn, Kidd's Hotel, still exists, at the head of Ullswater, to which fashion has not resorted and where kindness presides over the traveller's comfort. Close by also is a cosy nook called Glenridding, where, if you are a lover of solitude and peace, you may find an ideal abode. One house wherein lodging may be obtained was literally embowered in roses on that summer evening when first I strolled by the fragrant hay-fields on the Patterdale shore of Ullswater. The rose flourishes in wonderful luxuriance and profusion throughout Westmoreland and Cumberland. As you drive along the lonely roads your way will sometimes be, for many miles, between hedges that are bespangled with wild roses and with the silver globes of the laurel blossom, while around you the lonely mountains, bare of foliage save for matted grass and a dense growth of low ferns, tower to meet the clouds. It is a wild place, and yet there is a pervading spirit of refinement over it all,—as if Nature had here wrought her wonders in the mood of the finest art. And at the same time it is a place of infinite variety. The whole territory occupied by the lakes and mountains of this famous district is scarcely more than thirty miles square; yet within this limit, comparatively narrow, are comprised all possible beauties of land and water that the most passionate worshipper of natural loveliness could desire.

My first night in Patterdale was one of such tempest as sometimes rages in America about the time of the fall equinox. The wind shook the building. It was long after midnight when I went to rest, and the storm seemed to increase in fury as the night wore on. Torrents of rain were dashed against the windows. Great trees near by creaked and groaned beneath the strength of the gale. The cold was so severe that blankets were welcome. It was my first night in Wordsworth's country, and I thought of Wordsworth's lines:

> "There was a roaring in the wind all night;
> The rain came heavily and fell in floods."

The next morning was sweet with sunshine and gay with birds and flowers, and all semblance of storm and trouble seemed banished forever.

> "But now the sun is shining calm and bright,
> And birds are singing in the distant woods."

Wordsworth's poetry expresses the inmost soul of those lovely lakes and mighty hills, and no writer can hope to tread, save remotely and with reverent humility, in the footsteps of that magician. You understand Wordsworth better, however, and you love him more dearly, for having rambled over his consecrated ground. There was not a day when I did not, in some shape or another, meet with his presence. Whenever I was alone his influence came upon me as something unspeakably majestic and solemn. Once, on a Sunday, I climbed to the top of Place Fell [which is 2154 feet above the sea-level, while Scawfell Pike is 3210, and Helvellyn is 3118], and there, in the short space of two hours, I was thrice cut off by rainstorms from all view of the world beneath. Not a tree could I find on that mountain-top, nor any place of shelter from the blast and the rain, except when crouching beside the mound of rock at its summit, which in that country they call a "man." Not a living creature was visible, save now and then a lonely sheep, who stared at me for a moment and then scurried away. But when the skies cleared and the cloudy squadrons of the storm went careering over Helvellyn, I looked down into no less than fifteen valleys beautifully coloured by the foliage and the patches of cultivated land, each vale being sparsely fringed with little gray stone dwellings that seemed no more than card-houses, in those appalling depths. You think of Wordsworth, in such a place as that,—if you know his poetry. You cannot choose but think of him.

> "Who comes not hither ne'er shall know
> How beautiful the world below."

Yet somehow it happened that whenever friends joined in those rambles the great poet was sure to dawn upon us in a comic way. When we were resting on the bridge at the foot of Brothers Water, which is a little lake, scarcely more than a mountain tarn, lying between Ullswater and the Kirkstone Pass, some one recalled that Wordsworth had once rested there and written a poem about it. We were not all as devout admirers of the bard as I am, and certainly it is not every one of the great author's compositions that a lover of his genius would wish to hear quoted, under such circumstances. The Brothers Water poem is the one that begins "The cock is crowing, the stream is flowing," and I do not think that its insipidity is much relieved by its famous picture of the grazing cattle, "forty feeding like one." Henry Irving, not much given to enthusiasm about Wordsworth, heard those lines with undisguised merriment, and made a capital travesty of them on the spot. It is significant to remember, with reference to the inequality of Wordsworth, that on the day before he wrote "The cock is crowing," and at a place but a short distance from the Brothers Water bridge, he had written that peerless lyric about the daffodils,—"I wandered lonely as a cloud." Gowbarrow Park is the scene of that poem,—a place of ferns and hawthorns, notable for containing Lyulph's Tower, a romantic, ivy-clad lodge owned by the Duke of Norfolk, and Aira Force, a waterfall much finer than Lodore. Upon the lake shore in Gowbarrow Park you may still see the daffodils as Wordsworth saw them, a golden host, "glittering and dancing in the breeze." No one but a true poet could have made that perfect lyric, with its delicious close:

> "For oft, when on my couch I lie
> In vacant or in pensive mood,
> They flash upon that inward eye
> Which is the bliss of solitude:
> And then my heart with pleasure fills,
> And dances with the daffodils."

The third and fourth lines were written by the poet's wife, and they show that she was not a poet's wife in vain. It must have been in his "vacant mood" that he rested and wrote, on the bridge at Brothers Water. "I saw Wordsworth often when I was a child," said Frank Marshall [who had joined us at Penrith]; "he used to come to my father's house, Patterdale Hall, and once I was sent to the garden by Mrs. Wordsworth to call him to supper. He was musing there, I suppose. He had a long, horse-like face. I don't think I liked him. I said, 'Your wife wants you.' He looked down at me and he answered, 'My boy, you should say Mrs. Wordsworth, and not "your wife."' I looked up at him and I replied, 'She is your wife, isn't she?' Whereupon he said no more. I don't think he liked me either." We were going up Kirkstone Pass when Marshall told this story,—which seemed to bring the pensive and homely poet plainly before us. An hour later, at the top of the pass, while waiting in the old inn called the Traveller's Rest, which incorrectly proclaims itself the highest inhabited house in England, I spoke with an ancient, weather-beaten hostler, not wholly unfamiliar with the medicinal virtue of ardent spirits, and asked for his opinion of the great lake poet. "Well," he said, "people are always talking about Wordsworth, but I don't see much in it. I've read it, but I don't care for it. It's dry stuff—it don't chime." Truly there are all sorts of views, just as there are all sorts of people.

Mementos of Wordsworth are frequently encountered by the traveller among these lakes and fells. One of them, situated at the foot of Place Fell, is a rustic cottage that the poet once selected for his residence: it was purchased for him by Lord Lonsdale, as a partial indemnity for losses caused by an ancestor of his to Wordsworth's father. The poet liked the place, but he never lived there. The house somewhat resembles the Shakespeare cottage at Stratford,—the living-room being floored with stone slabs, irregular in size and shape and mostly broken by hard use. In a corner of the kitchen stands a fine carved oak cupboard, dark with age, inscribed with the date of the Merry Monarch, 1660.

What were the sights of those sweet days that linger still, and will always linger, in my remembrance? A ramble in the park of Patterdale Hall [the old name of the estate is Halsteads], which is full of American trees; a golden morning in Dovedale, with Irving, much like Jaques, reclined upon a shaded rock, half-way up the mountain, musing and moralising in his sweet, kind way, beside the brawling stream; the first prospect of Windermere, from above Ambleside,—a vision of heaven upon earth; the drive by Rydal Water, which has all the loveliness of celestial pictures seen in dreams; the glimpse of stately Rydal Hall and of the sequestered Rydal Mount, where Wordsworth so long lived and where he died; the Wishing Gate, where one of us, I know, wished in his heart that he could be young again and be wiser than to waste his youth in self-willed folly; the restful hours of observation and thought at delicious Grasmere, where we stood in silence at Wordsworth's grave and heard the murmur of Rotha singing at his feet; the lovely drive past

Matterdale, across the moorlands, with only clouds and rooks for our chance companions, and mountains for sentinels along our way; the ramble through Keswick, all golden and glowing in the afternoon sun, till we stood by Crosthwaite church and read the words of commemoration that grace the tomb of Robert Southey; the divine circuit of Derwent,—surely the loveliest sheet of water in England; the descent into the vale of Keswick, with sunset on the rippling crystal of the lake and the perfume of countless wild roses on the evening wind. These things, and the midnight talk about these things,—Irving, so tranquil, so gentle, so full of keen and sweet appreciation of them,—Bendall, so bright and thoughtful,—Marshall, so quaint and jolly, and so full of knowledge equally of nature and of books!—can never be forgotten. In one heart they are cherished forever.

Wordsworth is buried in Grasmere churchyard, close by the wall, on the bank of the little river Rotha. "Sing him thy best," said Matthew Arnold, in his lovely dirge for the great poet—

> "Sing him thy best! for few or none
> Hears thy voice right, now he is gone."

In the same grave with Wordsworth sleeps his devoted wife. Beside them rest the poet's no less devoted sister Dorothy, who died at Rydal Mount in 1855, aged 83, and his daughter, Dora, together with her husband Edward Quillinan, of whom Arnold wrote so tenderly:

> "Alive, we would have changed his lot,
> We would not change it now."

On the low gravestone that marks the sepulchre of Wordsworth are written these words: "William Wordsworth, 1850. Mary Wordsworth, 1859." In the neighbouring church a mural tablet presents this inscription:

"To the memory of William Wordsworth. A true poet
and philosopher, who by the special gift and calling
of Almighty God, whether he discoursed on man or
nature, failed not to lift up the heart to holy things,
tired not of maintaining the cause of the poor and
simple, and so in perilous times was raised up to be
a chief minister, not only of noblest poetry, but of
high and sacred truth. The memorial is raised here by
his friends and neighbours, in testimony of respect,
affection, and gratitude. Anno MDCCCLI."

A few steps from that memorable group will bring you to the
marble cross that marks the resting-place of Hartley Coleridge,
son of the great author of The Ancient Mariner, himself a poet
of exquisite genius; and close by is a touching memorial to
the gifted man who inspired Matthew Arnold's poems of The
Scholar-Gipsy and Thyrsis. This is a slab laid upon his mother's
grave, at the foot of her tombstone, inscribed with these words:

"In memory of Arthur Hugh Clough, some time
Fellow of Oriel College, Oxford, the beloved son of
James Butler and Anne Clough. This remembrance
in his own country is placed on his mother's grave by
those to whom life was made happy by his presence
and his love. He is buried in the Swiss cemetery at
Florence, where he died, November 13, 1861, aged 42.

"'So, dearest, now thy brows are cold
I see thee what thou art, and know
Thy likeness to the wise below,
Thy kindred with the great of old.'"

Southey rests in Crosthwaite churchyard, about half a mile
north of Keswick, where he died. They show you Greta Hall,
a fine mansion, on a little hill, enclosed in tall trees, which for

forty years, ending in 1843, was the poet's home. In the church is a marble figure of Southey, recumbent on a large stone sarcophagus. His grave is in the ground, a little way from the church, marked by a low flat tomb, on the end of which appears an inscription commemorative of a servant who had lived fifty years in his family and is buried near him. There was a pretty scene at this grave. When I came to it Irving was already there, and was speaking to a little girl who had guided him to the spot. "If any one were to give you a shilling, my dear," he said, "what would you do with it?" The child was confused and she murmured softly, "I don't know, sir." "Well," he continued, "if any one were to give you two shillings, what would you do?" She said she would save it. "But what if it were three shillings?" he asked, and each time he spoke he dropped a silver coin into her hand, till he must have given her more than a dozen of them. "Four—five—six—seven—what would you do with the money?" "I would give it to my mother, sir," she answered at last, her little face all smiles, gazing up at the stately, sombre stranger, whose noble countenance never looked more radiant than it did then, with gentle kindness and pleasure. It is a trifle to mention, but it was touching in its simplicity; and that amused group, around the grave of Southey, in the blaze of the golden sun of a July afternoon, with Skiddaw looming vast and majestic over all, will linger with me as long as anything lovely and of good report is treasured in my memory. Long after we had left the place I chanced to speak of its peculiar interest. "The most interesting thing I saw there," said Irving, "was that sweet child." I do not think the great actor was ever much impressed with the beauties of the lake poets.

Another picture glimmers across my dream,—a picture of peace and happiness which may close this rambling reminiscence of gentle days. We had driven up the pass between Glencoin and Gowbarrow, and had reached Matterdale, on our way toward Troutbeck station,—not the beautiful Windermere Troutbeck, but the less famous one. The road is lonely, but at Matterdale the traveller sees a few houses, and there our gaze was attracted by a gray church nestled in a hollow of the hillside. It stands sequestered in its place of graves, with bright greensward around it and a few trees. A faint sound of organ music floated from this sacred building and seemed to deepen the hush of the summer wind and shed a holier calm upon the lovely solitude. We dismounted and silently entered the church. A youth and a maiden, apparently lovers, were sitting at the organ,—the youth playing and the girl listening, and looking with tender trust and innocent affection into his face. He recognised our presence with a kindly nod, but went on with the music. I do not think she saw us at all. The place was full of soft, warm light streaming through the stained glass of Gothic windows and fragrant with perfume floating from the hay-fields and the dew-drenched roses of many a neighbouring hedge. Not a word was spoken, and after a few moments we departed, as silently as we had come. Those lovers will never know what eyes looked upon them that day, what hearts were comforted with the sight of their happiness, or how a careworn man, three thousand miles away, fanning upon his hearthstone the dying embers of hope, now thinks of them with tender sympathy, and murmurs a blessing on the gracious scene which their presence so much endeared.

A CHAPTER FROM
*Grey Days and Gold
in England and Scotland*, 1891

Printed in Great Britain
by Amazon

13006253R00105